LOCOMOTIVE PANORAMA
Vol. I

LOCOMOTIVE PANORAMA

Volume I

by

E. S. COX

M.I. MECH. E. M.I. LOCO. E.

LONDON

IAN ALLAN LTD

First published 1965
This edition 1974

ISBN 07110 0543 5

Published by Ian Allan Ltd, Shepperton, Surrey
and printed in the United Kingdom by
Biddles Ltd, Guildford, Surrey

CONTENTS

List of Tables

List of Diagrams

List of Photographs

(By the author unless otherwise stated)

PLATE NO.

PREFACE

Yet another locomotive book raises the question as to when will the well run dry. Excellent recent publications have covered history and practice, classified by individual railways, by chief mechanical engineers and by types of locomotives. Anything these lack may be sought by the student in the files of the railway and technical press, while the societies, manned as they are by devoted enthusiasts, gather up the crumbs which only painstaking investigation can identify. On another plane, the Proceedings of the Institutions of Mechanical, Electrical, and Locomotive Engineers yield a rich harvest. While, therefore, there can be little new to be said upon the subject, the manner of its telling can still be varied and made to yield a further measure of interest.

Apart from the case of the professional institutions, the greater part of this large output on locomotive development has been the work of writers outside the railway rolling stock departments. Dedicated, knowledgeable, and enjoying the close friendship of, responsible railway officers, they must nevertheless assemble their material as onlookers, even if as such they traditionally see most of the game. To those railway people who have themselves borne the heat and burden of the day, things often appear slightly different, and it could be that to see matters from the other side as well, might leaven the ultimate judgement upon past events.

To balance the product of lay authorship, there lies the meagre contribution of railway engineers themselves—and with good reason. To carry responsibility in a large department takes of the best that they can give, and fully occupies their time. Sufficient 'writing' to last them a lifetime arises in the endless memoranda, reports, and correspondence, all part of the daily grind. The more enthusiastic possessing some gift of tongues, prepare papers for the Institutions and that is usually the end of it. They are content that others record from the remainder anything worth recording. Thus the number of books from this source is small, and the works of Mason, Lynes and Holcroft are all that readily come to mind covering recent years.

By good fortune, I have been close to the seat of locomotive design policy throughout the whole of my career which has taken me from apprentice and junior draughtsman on one of the lesser of the old constituent railways, to Assistant Chief Mechanical Engineer of British Railways, about as high up the ladder as any primarily design man can hope to get. Within that period I have kept diaries, notes, photographs and diagrams. Supplemented by memory, these combine to form a record. It would be a pity to allow this to dissolve away without presentation. Hence this book!

Although the articles of association of the Institution of Locomotive Engineers define locomotive engineering as inclusive of all vehicles which move on rails, and although in the latter part of my career carriage and wagon design and development has played as large a part as that of locomotives, I have confined myself to locomotives in order to produce a more coherent narrative. By its period the story is mainly concerned with steam, but reaches also over the great change in motive power of more recent years. I have passed from Lancashire and Yorkshire, to London Midland and Scottish, and finally to British Railways and have at one time and another been absorbed, co-ordinated, amalgamated, nationalised and abolished! Having served under nine chief mechanical engineers or their equivalent, my work has taken me to more than twenty countries throughout the world, with all the diverse technical and human contacts arising from such travel.

In 1942 I read a paper " A Modern Locomotive History—Ten Years' Development on the L.M.S.—1923 to 1932 " which recorded some of this experience over a particular period. I have thought that it might be of interest to amplify and expand this over a wider span, and to combine with it a measure of personal experiences sufficient to indicate what form a career in locomotive engineering could take over the days that have now gone.

Faced with the choice of the level at which the tale should be told I have tried to steer a middle course between mere anecdote on the one hand and a technical treatise on the other. Names and numbers appear only incidentally, and lists of dimensions and other data are absent where they have been well presented elsewhere. The facts which are stated are I hope sufficiently accurate; the opinions are solely my own.

Not to refer to the many personalities who have shaped the trend of development over so many years would leave untold one of the most important aspects, and this book is freely scattered with the names of both the great and the lowly. It is clearly impossible to refer to all, but I have tried to sketch those mentioned as realistically as I can in the light in which I knew them. If by attention to this specialised interest I have by default done less than justice to their stature in other fields, I apologise profoundly and offer in excuse that this is no biography.

Finally, every engine diagram which is reproduced is a copy of an actual diagram officially prepared at the time, and I have tried as far as possible to illustrate the text by photographs hitherto unpublished. My grateful acknowledgements are due to my chiefs both past and present, and to my many colleagues both inside and outside the railway with whom I have experienced the history which I have now endeavoured to set down.

Among this succession of names too numerous to display, I should especially like to mention Roland Bond, who has been kind enough to read the text and make helpful comments, A. H. Edleston of the CM & EE Department at Derby and originally from Horwich who has given much assistance in the seeking out and preparation of the diagrams, and J. F. Thomas of Bury for putting me in touch with George Smith, who over 80 years old at the time of writing, has made available to me a selection of L. & Y. photographs which he took before the First World War. Lastly my thanks are due to my daughter, Diana, and to my secretary, Brenda McLennan, who gave up so much of their spare time to the typing of the manuscript and the handling of the correspondence.

E. S. Cox.

I

Lancashire and Yorkshire

1917-1921

THE year is 1917, third year of World War I, so different from the last war in the more terrible nature of the overseas battles and in the relative normality of the whole segments of life at home. Picture, without too much sympathy, the arrival of the author on a cloudy afternoon of October at the single open platform of Horwich Station. In this town were the locomotive workshops of the Lancashire & Yorkshire Railway, 12th in mileage among the 16 main line railway companies which straddled Great Britain at that time. Having journeyed thence successively through Wigan and Blackrod, no garden cities, the skies looming over Rivington Pike, and the deserted air of a small Lancashire manufacturing town on Sunday afternoon, were far from cheering to the traveller. His welcome into 'Ma' Miller's digs in Fox Street was kindly meant, so far as the other young men there resident were concerned, but the general air of "what on earth have you come here for?" was depressing. Contemplation of the plunge which had to be made on the morrow into the unknown world of a large engineering works, finally lowered his spirits into his boots. Who has not had similar feelings upon their first entry into the world at large, away from the sheltered routine of school and home?

As a matter of fact, little sympathy need be spent upon this doleful advent for your author had brought it upon himself. With no relatives or connections in engineering, let alone in Railways, he could most sensibly have followed in his father's footsteps and worked towards the Civil Service entrance exams. From nowhere at all had come a love of locomotives and their environment, starting with toy trains, and a still vaguely remembered vision of something in red with outside frames and cranks in Manningham, nearest station to where he lived when memory awoke. At his next home on the Lancashire coast, and through his schooldays, there was a ceaseless growth of self generated interest. Discovery of the "Railway Magazine" and "The Locomotive", and the acquiring of sundry books, Charles Lake's "The World's Locomotives"[1] with its general arrangement drawings being the most treasured, led inevitably to entry for the school hobby show of such items as "Design for a 4–6–2 locomotive—Elevation and Cross Section" by E. S. Cox, aged 16. The world of engine spotters, and the considerable activity which supports them today was then unknown, and in any case all this increasing interest was directed much more to *how* it works than to lists of numbers. The latter were far from scorned, however, but were difficult to come by.

There came the day when parents could hardly ignore the urge. The Headmaster was unhelpful for he clearly thought of engineering as crazy for one of his classical scholars, not too bright at maths, who had been renowned for his unhandy work in the school's woodworking class. One day schoolfriend Baxter produced a Chambers Encyclopaedia which indicated that most railway companies ran systems of premium apprenticeships for aspirants having a certain standard of education. An interview and payment of a £50 premium began a chain reaction which led directly to my being handed over in due course to leading hand Sam Heath, who was in charge of a group of miscellaneous small lathes worked by apprentices in the middle of Horwich Works Machine Shop.

At that time the Lancashire & Yorkshire Railway, although smaller than some, was not without a certain measure of importance, lying 5th in the number of its locomotives, just above the Great Northern and just below the North Eastern. It is no figment of memory to recall that it stood then, and had been standing for a number of years a good deal higher than its mere size warranted. In the first place, there was the coming to fruition of the work of one of the great names in locomotive history, John Aspinall. Although no longer himself in harness, he and his successors had pioneered a consistent large engine policy for the more important duties in conjunction with a highly standardised range of smaller types for general work. Nearly the whole of the locomotive stock as it had stood in 1886 when Horwich Works had opened, had been replaced, consequently the relatively modern fleet was of a much lower average age than that which served other railways.

Secondly Horwich was the youngest but one of the major locomotive works in the country. In addition to layout and equipment uncluttered by legacies from the past, Horwich developed under Aspinall's guidance policies of standardisation and interchangeable parts ahead of its time. Moreover, under Hughes it had

[1] Published by Percival Marshall, 1904.

pioneered the high degree superheater in this country. The railway and works thus attracted to itself men of engineering substance. It is interesting to recall that Sir Nigel Gresley, Sir Henry Fowler, and J. P. Crouch, sometime C.M.E. of the Central Argentine, were at different times L. & Y. men. Plate 1 taken from an old print bearing the date 1912, displays an array of talent which illustrates the point. Then again this railway was a pioneer in electrification. Its 18½ mile line from Liverpool to Southport, converted to this form of traction in 1903, provided the first inter-city electric services in this country as distinct from purely suburban lines. Until the end of its separate existence, there was always a very active and forward looking electric traction department.

Two books by Eric Mason[1,2] have, to a very detailed extent, described the locomotive stock of the L. & Y. as well as its physical features and train services. His second book has captured the atmosphere of Horwich and its works, and of life there as it was at that time, so there is a great deal which it is possible to omit from the present chronicle.

The present aspect of the works as it still largely was in 1917 has been fully set out in the Railway Magazine for August, 1913. The machine shop under the foremanship of a real old character, Jimmy Crewe, was a maze of shafts and belts (Plate 2). Individual electric drive of machine tools was a rarity and two large vertical engines, supplied with steam from the works' Lancashire boilers, covered the South wall of each main bay, driving the shafting through bevel gears. When any breakdown occurred half the shop had a holiday—much to the joy of the apprentices! There was a lot of wartime fuse and shell production spread round the works, and women operatives, still something of a nine days wonder, were now firmly established on this work. The tool room also undertook a great deal of special gauge production for the Ministry of Munitions, under its foreman, James Walkden. This laid the foundation of the leadership at Horwich that subsequently led to the introduction of more advanced methods into the construction and repair of locomotive components.[3]

The first week at work was pure joy tinged with apprehension. At last one was really on the spot surrounded by little else than locomotives and the means of building and repairing them. New boys were usually started on a little group of simple lathes turning

[1] *The Lancashire and Yorkshire Railway in the Twentieth Century*—Eric Mason (Ian Allan 1954).

[2] *My Life with Locomotives*—" Rivington " (Ian Allan 1962).

[3] " Limit Gauging in Horwich Locomotive Shops "—(*Railway Engineer*, Oct. 1923).

out roofing bar bolts. Even these humble objects held glamour as part of the finished engine, and if any later student of design does not recognise this item, it must be recalled that direct stays connecting the roof of inner fireboxes to the roundtop outer wrapper plate were not then commonplace. On all of the smaller L. & Y. engines the crown was self-supported by a series of cast steel girders distributed laterally across the top of the inner box and secured to the latter by numerous set bolts inserted from inside the firebox—these were the roofing bar bolts.

Three trade apprentices 'Tup', 'Gaff' and 'Ainy'—their real names long forgotten—shared the job with three 'premiums', Frank Mason, 'Ike' Lucas and myself. The thrill of thrills was to escape down to the South end of the works where the incoming locomotives for repair were stabled. There were always anything up to 20 locomotives standing on these remote sidings, and there one could climb in and out of the different cabs and experience intense satisfaction only mitigated by the fear of being found out. Besides the hazard of roving foremen, there was the blasphemous reception if one climbed up on to one of the footplates already tenanted by some of the men foregathered for a smoke; an indulgence still officially banned inside the shops. Fortunately this latter occurrence was rare, for an inner firebox of the parked spare boilers in another part of the works was usually judged a safer hide-out. The Saturday morning shift from 6.0 a.m. to 10.15 a.m. without a break was the accepted time for visiting. On my first such day I was taken over to the erecting shop to meet Eric Mason—no relation to my workmate on 'roofers'—who was one day to be the author of the books referred to above.

Apprentices who were specially interested in locomotives and who could distinguish one type from another were regarded as cranks. As I had already disclosed these proclivities to my fellows in the digs what more natural than for me to be taken, at the earliest moment, to meet the arch crank himself!

Mason could talk locomotives till the cows came home. He had a collection of railway photographs he had taken himself, and a manuscript list giving minute details of all L. & Y. locomotives for which I greatly envied him. Lists of numbers were worth more then than now, for one of the minor mysteries of most pre-grouping railways was the sacred nature of engine numbers. Railway traffic was still expanding and locomotive stocks increased annually in sympathy. It was simply not done to allocate further numbers to new constructions from the top end of the series, until every blank vacated by an engine broken up had been painstakingly filled. The American 'folie de grandeur' of numbering a new locomotive 9000 on a railroad such as the Union Pacific, having a total stock of locomotives almost exactly equal to that of the L. & Y., was considered quite indecent. Due to the former practice, on the L. & Y. and on its neighbour the L.N.W.R., identical engines constructed consecutively could bear widely differing numbers. It resulted that if a wire arrived at headquarters to say, for example, that No. 627 had dropped its motion (i.e. valve gear) onto the track at Hindley, a quite exceptional memory was called for to diagnose the engine type involved without recourse to the stock list.

In the second week, the triple ordeal began. Illustrations of the facts of life were set up in chalk on an adjacent column to see if one winced, and age old clichés were trotted out such as sending one for a bucket of steam, or for a lead hammer to be hardened. Most insidious of all were searching questions about one's family life and background. The purpose here was to find some weakness, some sensibility or inhibition which could be exploited thereafter to the huge joy of these cheerful young ruffians. If they were lucky and you were not, this might even end in fastening upon you a juicy nick-name which would last the length of your apprenticeship and beyond.

Training schools and apprentice supervisors were still of the future. All that was undertaken on behalf of premium apprentices generally before and during World War I was to put them through machine fitting and erecting shops, and to turn them out at 21 qualified as fitters. To achieve this end they were worked from 6.0 a.m. to 5.30 p.m., and were encouraged by a nominal starting pay of 7/- per week. By 1917 wartime inflation was under way and my take home pay actually began at 21/8d., a sum sufficient to pay board and lodging.

Nobody received more than a few minutes' instruction at a time from leading hand or mate. Turning on the lathe, and later, chipping and filing on the fitting bench had to be picked up by observation, trial and error, and the application of such mother wit as one might possess. But what was learned in this rough and ready way was remembered and one picked up a lot of the art of dealing with human beings in the process. The normal time-table of job changes was upset in wartime by the calling up of all apprentices when they reached 19. My sojourn in the machine shop was thus foreshortened. After passing from 'roofers' to a general purpose lathe on miscellaneous turning, followed by a spell on a fitting bench, I was within ten months posted to the erecting shop.

This shop, a quarter of a mile long, was presided over by a rather austere chief foreman, F. P. Wilde. It was divided, like Gaul, into three parts, of which the southernmost built new engines, and repaired the larger types. At the date of my advent No. 1529 had just been completed—a large boiler non-superheated 0–8–0 (Plate 3). This was a reflection of wartime austerity, for a batch of 20 such locomotives was sandwiched between similar superheated engines built during 1917, and further superheater engines which began again at the end of 1918. My first job was on Martin's repair pit on No. 154, a small boilered 0–8–0. In little more than a month the same affect of the call up brought another shift, this time into the central section of the shop which dealt with the smaller types, and in particular onto the stripping pit in that shop. This work was rough and very dirty but under an excellent leading hand, Robinson, and with a rapid succession of engines of various types to pull apart, a great deal could be learned here of the anatomy of the locomotives and the effects of different features of design.

Considering erecting shop work generally there was much more hard work in those days, to an extent unthinkable now. For example, when it was necessary to cut out an arc in a footplate supporting angle to clear the wheels, vertical hand sawcuts were made in the flange of varying depth, and about ½″ apart. The material was then chipped out by hammer and chisel, section by section, the rough surface so formed being finally filed smooth. This would take a few minutes with an oxy-flame cutter today. No portable grinders radiused off the sharp edges of coupling and connecting rods as they came off the milling machines. They had to be chipped and filed all the way round to give the required radius. Most terrifying of all to apprentices entering this shop was their introduction to the big hammer and set, used for driving bolts or splitting large nuts. Sometimes in order to reach a seemingly inaccessible position it was necessary to strike the end of a slender bar held up by one's mate. One learned new and fantastic uses of the English language if, before confidence was gained, one missed the target! Among the heaviest jobs was the bedding in of axle-boxes. In later days of steam, machining of both axle journal and boxes became sufficiently accurate for the one to be assembled to the other without any fitting. Then, however, each box had to be manoeuvred up and down an inclined plank while the white metal bearing was successively scraped and tried on the journal. This process was repeated several times before the tell-tale red lead indicated that contact between the two was established over a sufficient area. This crude mating process was far from finished when the engine went out. Trial trips near the works, and light duties for a few days at the home shed completed the procedure. It is small wonder that hot bearings were an epidemic disease of most pre-World War I railways, especially when, as was too often the case excessive bearing loads and poor facilities for lubrication were combined with so inconsistent a means of winning the required bearing surface.

The locomotives themselves have been described class by class, and number by number, by Mason in conjunction with the services which they worked. They numbered 1596 at the start of this chronicle of which some 400 were large by the standards of the time, and the remainder were relatively small. Compared with other lines such as the North Western and Midland the L. & Y. was unusual in having no medium sized engines and no old crocks. Although its large engines were often seen on light trains, as was obviously necessary in building up daily rosters consisting of many separate short runs, there were enough of them to cover all the heavier workings. For this reason double heading, whether of passenger or freight trains, was almost unknown. In my own observation this only occurred for a short period when practically all of the Hughes 4–6–0s were withdrawn in the months before rebuilding. I exclude from this definition the attachment of a small 4–4–0 which gave banking assistance to the heavier trains tackling the mountainous eastward gradients starting from the platform end of Manchester Victoria.

That there were no old crocks to speak of was the result of Aspinall's policies already mentioned. As Ahrons has reminded us, in writing in the same year as this story starts,[1] of the 673 engines existing in 1876 there were only two still at work in 1917. Also some 530 further engines, their successors of 1877 to 1887, had also either completed their existence or had been radically altered in the same time.

George Hughes mentioned in one of his papers, that in 1889 there were 29 types of passenger and 26 types of goods engines at work. By 1917 this variety had been reduced to 16 separate designs of locomotive, thus forming a highly standardised fleet.

This last phrase requires, however, some qualification. The basis of the 16 types was highly standardised in boiler dimensions,

[1] " Locomotive & Train working in the latter part of the 19th Century—Lancashire Yorkshire Railway "—E. L. Ahrons. (*Railway Magazine* Vol. XLI 1917).

wheel diameters, rods and motion, and in fittings of all kinds. But this railway was an inveterate re-builder and certain differences already introduced for traffic reasons became greatly expanded by the advent of superheating. Thus within the stock of 330 2–4–2 Radial Tank Engines there were no less than 12 sub-variants covering long and short bunkers, $17\frac{1}{2}''$, 18″ or $20\frac{1}{2}''$ dia. cylinders, Belpaire or Round Top fireboxes, saturated or superheated, the latter with Schmidt or Hughes 'Top & Bottom' versions. There were also flat, back to back, and piston valves. The 484 0–6–0 goods tender engines partook of most of these modifications plus some with twin plug superheaters, and the 235 0–8–0 coal engines added large and small boilers, Robinson superheaters, and compounding to the mélange. As pioneers in the application of the high degree superheaters in this country the L. & Y. first applied the 'Schmidt' arrangement, but in those days there was an almost pathological resistance to proprietary or patented articles. Thus most C.M.E.s at the dawn of superheating promptly set about inventing—adapting would be a better word—variants of the 'Schmidt' idea to which they could attach their own name, and in some cases draw their own royalties. This 'invention' often consisted of little more than varying the means by which the elements were attached to the header, but this sufficed. Thus 'Schmidt' was replaced by 'Robinson' on the principle that short of one's own design it was not quite so disgraceful to adopt that of a brother C.M.E. The true Hughes products were first the Twin Plug, and then the Top and Bottom Header arrangements, both described by Mason. In both of these the large tubes, in banks of 2 or 3 rows according to the degree of superheat sought, were arranged in two vertical banks, one on each side of the boiler barrel, and steampipes as such were dispensed with in the smokebox. The earlier 'Plug' design was a horror to strip down, but the Top and Bottom arrangement was quite satisfactory, although technically it had no advantage at all over the Schmidt.

A curious backwater of locomotive history is that the L. & Y. was the first to apply together high degree superheat and long travel piston valves, the arrangement which in combination produced the modern steam locomotive in its final form. It did not however develop or even recognise the treasure it had found. The first four 4–4–0 locos. to be fitted with superheaters in 1908, Nos. 1098, 1104, 1105 and 1110 also had inside Walschaert gear giving 6″ travel to piston valves having $1\frac{1}{2}''$ lap (Plate 4). These engines, for the relatively short time they remained in original condition, put up some quite breathtaking performances for their size and were for a period given 'Atlantic' duties. However three out of the four had been converted to short travel Joy's valve gear by 1921, and the fourth was broken up after an accident in 1924. The markedly inferior performance of the altered engines was accepted as the price to be paid for release from lubrication and undue wear problems in the steam chests. Until the end of steam, piston valve lubrication has continued as a problem, so it is not surprising that in the very first attempt at longer valve travel with high temperature steam this difficulty loomed prohibitively large.

Outstanding among these locomotives were the 'Atlantics' of which a stud of forty was the mainstay of the important passenger traffic (Plate 5). From the turn of the century they had been associated with the hourly non-stop service between Liverpool and Manchester, which was the Company's showpiece. Until the war-time decelerations set in, twelve trains had left each city throughout the day at a fixed number of minutes past the hour. The run was scheduled to take 40 minutes over 36½ steeply graded miles, including sections as severe as 1 in 70. A high power to weight ratio was provided, parent of all high speed services, whatever the form of motive power. With trains of three to six light coaches six horse-power per ton sufficed to make the run possible in 37 minutes giving margin enough for a high degree of punctuality (Plate 6).

So here, 50 years and more ago was a pocket of modernisation containing high speed, frequency, punctuality and a time-table so contrived that the public need not refer to a time-table at all. Two wars, economic depression and the rise of the road motor changed for ever the climate in which train services of that kind could be justified over that particular route. As an example of the public's complete dependence upon railways during the 1919 railway strike I instance the occasion of a return from Horwich to my home in Blundellsands, 24 miles as the crow flies. The only available means of public transport other than the railway was the electric tramcar. I made the whole journey by the latter means in 7 hours, making a wide sweep over Southern Lancashire through Bolton, Atherton, St. Helens, Prescott, and Liverpool, patronising 6 different tramway authorities and journeying some 40 miles. Although the total cost was only 2/6 it was an ordeal of bodily discomfort as well as of time wasting which nobody in his right mind would incur when the railway was available.

Beside the noble 'Atlantics' the various 4–4–0's were a rather pallid lot, excepting only the first four superheated conversions in their original condition to which reference has already been made. The real breadwinning on the railway was undertaken by the hard core of 1114 2–4–2 Tank and 0–6–0 Goods engines, both tender and tank. Cheap to build and simple to repair their hearts were stout enough to tackle all that was offered within their capacity and sometimes beyond it. Some of them were to last for 40 years ahead of their time we are now talking about. On the other hand the 0–8–0's and especially the large boilered ones, although sufficiently powerful, were rather undershod as to bearings, so that they found little favour after the demise of the L. & Y. Of the little group numbered from 1629 to 1639, on the building of which I was to perspire so freely when I returned to the erecting shop in 1920, the majority were broken up by 1936. One of them on which I actually worked, No. 1636, lasted however until 1950. I think it must have been the experience of putting up inside motion work on these engines on hot August afternoons which predisposed me against inside cylinders for the whole of my designing career!

Included in the locomotive stock there were however one complete failure, and one near-failure. The former was a series of 20 large 2–6–2 tank engines which had been designed in Hoy's time and built in 1903 (Plate 7). These were of a capacity which should have proved most useful, as was demonstrated in later years by the success of the Fowler 2–6–4 Tanks when they came to these lines. Tried at first on the Liverpool to Southport line just as electrification was coming on, and later on the Oldham line, these 2–6–2T's simply would not stay on the road. The geometric layout of the leading radial truck was defective, and the provision of the flangeless tyres on the intermediate coupled wheels did not help.

I never learned why the company preferred to leave these engines unaltered and to eke out their time so unproductively over many years doing shunting and banking duties and working short trips for which they were eminently unsuitable and uneconomic. A bogie could have replaced the radial truck at the front end and although this would have meant inclining the cylinders, there was ample room under the boiler to do this by the provision of a new leading frame section. A sketch, still in my possession, on these lines, which I had the temerity to make and show to Gass, the senior draughtsman, met with a particularly wintery reception!

The near failure was what should have been the pride of the fleet, namely the 4-cylinder saturated 4–6–0 (Plate 8). There were 20 of these (what magic there seemed to be for the old company in a series of 20) and their performance, shortcomings and maintenance difficulties have been graphically described by Mason, who in his own person experienced the full brunt of trying to keep them going. It was only on one or two of the York trains that their extra capacity over the 'Atlantics' was really needed. Although they could do the run from Manchester to Liverpool in 40 minutes with a substantial load, the only recorded efficiency test with them indicated a coal consumption of 7 lbs. per DBHP hour, an all time 'high' amongst such records as I have seen. Unlike the case of the Tank engine, here a bold decision was taken to make such an extensive rebuild as almost to constitute a new design, and it is on this that I cut my teeth as a draughtsman in due course.

The main features were the new cylinders and outside Walschaert gear. The former had straight ports and generously proportioned piston valves, while the latter provided a long travel of $6\frac{3}{8}''$, although the steam lap was only moderate at $1\frac{3}{16}''$. When I started my first spell in the Drawing Office in 1919 a large scale arrangement drawing of cylinders and valve gear had already been completed, and it was from this, starting with a steam chest cover and eventually including liners, valves, pistons, valve gear parts, rods, and wheels, that I picked up one component after another for detailing into the form of shop production drawings. A happy exercise unknown today rounded off each job in the form of painting the shop copies in all the colours of the rainbow to indicate the material, grey for cast iron, blue for steel, yellow for brass and so on. I was too junior to find out just who it was who had produced the basic thinking for this redesign which by inspection contained evidence that somebody had studied contemporary American practice in these matters. It may have been the chief who had in fact visited the U.S.A. in 1905 but I was already disabused of my innocent schoolboy belief that 'designed by X' printed in the description of a new locomotive necessarily meant that Mr. X with his own fair hand had drawn out the principal lineaments of what was ascribed to him. My further involvement with this locomotive is referred to in the next chapter but suffice it to say here that the first rebuild was turned out in 1920, and that it established at once with very little teething trouble a standard of achievement far higher than anything seen on the parent line up to that time. By 1922, out of the original 20, 15 converted engines averaged 50·2 lbs. of coal per mile, while the 5 unconverted, now relegated to less onerous duties, burned 65·2 lbs. per mile.

What else is to be said about this vanished stock of Horwich locomotives? They were all clean down to the humblest saddle tank—it just never occurred to anyone that locomotives could be left dirty and still work satisfactorily. During World War I large numbers of women in the voluminous overalls appropriate to the time were recruited at all the sheds for engine cleaning. A minor and curious fact was that this railway was the first to recognise that it was very sensible to drive a locomotive from a sitting position. Cabs all over Great Britain were so arranged that drivers must stand up to see forward and to drive. Windows were raised high, regulator handles pointed upwards, and brake handles were near the roof all to force the stance which was widely believed to spell alertness and safety. To sit was to sleep, to be sloppy, to endanger life and limb. Aspinall in 1899 designed the cab of the 'Atlantics' round the sitting position, so much so that his engines were actually awkward to drive standing up (Plate 9). All the large engines followed the same arrangement, but it was many years before it became commonplace and eventually universal. Even to this day the standing tradition lingers, and of all modern diesel and electric locos., those on the Southern Region alone are designed so as to be capable of being driven standing as well as sitting. In such curious by-ways do the remnants of social habits and belief linger on into the present.

Another curiosity only, I believe, to be found on the L. & Y. was the practice on all of the large Hughes engines of lagging the smoke-box. This certainly avoided paint blisters and rusty patches such as can occur where only a thin wrapper-sheet separates the hot gases from the atmosphere. This practice was part of the then prevalent idea of good appearance. This consisted of ensuring as smooth and unfussy an exterior as possible, but it led to some practices such as running the blower pipes, the ejector steam supply and exhaust pipes through the boiler barrel—a good arrangement when all was tight but the very devil if joints became defective at front tubeplate or backplate.

The electric train services have been referred to and warrant a slight digression. In the absence of alternative road transport other than tramcars the train service was magnificent. Stopping trains left Liverpool every 10 minutes throughout the day for Hall Road $7\frac{1}{2}$ miles out, of which every second train went on to Southport in 37 minutes. Once an hour a non-stop train ran direct in 25 minutes and during rush hours there were six more semi-fast trains each way. At other hourly intervals a through service ran from Southport to the southern terminus of the Liverpool Overhead Railway at Dingle, connecting the Mersey dockland directly with the coastal towns.

This operating cornucopia reached its zenith in 1914, was reduced during the war for fuel and staff economy, and never recovered thereafter as the expanding Ribble bus services creamed off all of the inner suburban work.

The rolling stock consisted of 60 motor cars and 92 trailers (Plates 10 & 11). The majority of the former weighed 47 tons, carried four 150 h.p. traction motors and huge tramcar type controllers dealing with the full line voltage, which was carried down the train. Twenty of them were arranged for multiple unit working in the modern manner but in practice were used only with fixed formation trains. Four of these motor cars had four 250 h.p. motors. The trailer cars carried 103 seated passengers at a tare weight of 24·75 tons giving 538 lbs. per seat. Of steel and wood construction these latter vehicles offered a weight per seat not greatly bettered by many modern designs in light alloy.

The most heroic feature of design of all of these vehicles was their 10 ft. width in conjunction with a straight sided profile. The civil engineers had been persuaded to set back platforms and adjust bridge clearances to permit this ample width which gave comfortable seating to three and two seats on either side of the centre gangway—so unlike the sardine-like posture demanded by today's standard vehicle of 9 ft. width.

To anyone who only knows the present semi-tube train type of stock now in use on this line, with its parsimonious shutting off of current half way between stations, the performance of the original vehicles before 1914 would be an eye-opener. Although vacuum brake was used deceleration was vigorous and very sharp station stops were assured by sergeant major like guards, two to each train, who carried out a ruthless campaign to force passengers to leave the cars by the front door in the direction of travel so that loading could take place simultaneously from the rear.

While rolling stock is being mentioned the contrast provided by the steam hauled stock must also be referred to. Although some more modern coaches were appearing the norm was still a low roofed vehicle mounted on short wheel base bogies with generous clearances under light wooden bodies. Travelling in these down to Liverpool at 80 m.p.h. was a terrifying experience never quite forgotten. Horsehair upholstery tortured youthful legs and naked batswing gaslights, still in wide use, only served to make darkness visible. Where incandescent gas lights were provided water in the pipes could lead to ' blobbing ' of the light, a condition more trying to the eyes than was dimness itself.

All this, and more, was accepted by a public who, remembering old and less enlightened days, were quite unaware of the standards of amenity which it would one day demand.

At this stage something should be said regarding the various personalities who were engaged in the mechanical engineering activities at Horwich. The leader was George Hughes, the Chief Mechanical Engineer since 1904 who, in such a small compact railway, was no remote figure. He was one of the few chiefs I have known who was well liked by his colleagues and assistants close at hand as he was by those more remote from him including the workmen. These latter visited their very human spleen on foremen and sub-chiefs in a perfectly normal way, but at any rate in my experience, were unusually well disposed to Hughes himself. This was no mystery for he was the embodiment of level headed common-sense without temperament or temper. Living on the hilltop between Horwich and Bolton he played his part in the works and office social occasions, and was frequently seen, if not spoken to, by every man, woman and boy on the establishment.

At work he divided his time between Horwich and Hunts Bank, Manchester; at the latter office he discharged his duties to the General Manager and presided over the motive power part of his kingdom, his vice regent in this domain being the somewhat shadowy person of F. W. Attock. His sway also extended over F. E. Gobey in charge of the carriage and wagon works out at Newton Heath.

By training and earlier experiences Hughes was in essence a workshop man and his book on locomotive construction written in 1896[1] was a stepping stone on his way to eminence. His two papers in 1909 and 1910 to the Institution of Mechanical Engineers[2,3], described in a practical manner locomotive development for which he had been responsible. Although hardly a great engineer he was certainly a competent one, ahead of rather than behind contemporary thought and practice. A man of strong personality, he could command in an effortless manner. Although anything but taciturn, Hughes was a man who wasted few words, and whether in a lecture,

[1] " The Construction of the Modern Locomotive "—George Hughes (*Spon* 1896).
[2] " Locomotives Designed and Built at Horwich "—George Hughes (*Proceedings* Inst. Mech. Engs. 1909).
[3] " Compounding and Superheating on Horwich Locomotives "—George Hughes (*Proceedings* Inst. Mech. Engs. 1910).

a speech on a social occasion or in personal contact, his utterances were short and to the point. In this connection his rather nasal voice was a gift to local humourists who would imitate his 'bon mots' before suitable audiences.

His incursions into the Drawing Office although not rare, were mercifully brief. The silence and tension in the office when the big man was at one of the boards was an unnatural phenomenon of which one could soon have enough. Happily, both by his personality and the gradual mellowing of the years, conditions were no longer as harsh as in days well remembered by the oldest draughtsmen. Between Aspinall's entering in at the top door and his exit at the bottom door, no man knew that he would still retain his job after the transit, should his demeanour or his work give offence.

While the principal assistants at Horwich were very far from being lay figures the personality of the chief loomed far more closely over all that went on in those days, and a brief footnote on these others must suffice. H. E. O'Brien, combined the jobs of assistant chief and works manager. Although a trained mechanical engineer he had been in charge of Lancashire coast electrification in 1903, and among his general responsibilities he retained a special interest in electrical matters. He was that *rara avis* in railway engineering circles, an old Etonian, and also a member of the Institute of Civil Engineers. In his latter capacity he summoned to his office on one occasion a number of we youngsters and more or less commanded us to apply for studentship in that Institution. Obediently some of us did so—it took years for us to realise that our chosen mechanical career was most unlikely to qualify us for eventual membership of of the Civils—and I at any rate quietly bowed out in due course.

On the design side was J. R. Billington, for whom I was to work more closely than for any of the others until his untimely death in 1925. Of humble Fylde coast parentage, and of short stature and slight build, Billington had a brilliant academic brain. From an early age he had marked himself for recognition by gaining distinction in the educational field. As Chief Draughtsman he controlled not only the steam locomotive office, but also the electrical design office, in which it must be said his greater personal interest lay. He did not suffer fools gladly and could be sharp and acid on occasion; however he was a born teacher and loved to impart his knowledge to those who would listen. I owe a great deal to his memory.

As deputy there was Edward Gass, the leading draughtsman. Of incredible thinness, his bow ties and spats produced a natty appearance not general in the office as a whole. A competent but not original designer he was a kindly man with very little sense of humour and I fear some of us at the junior end were a sore trial to him.

These were the 'bosses', but what of the mass of workmen, leading hands and foremen with whom one passed the days of one's apprenticeship, and from whom one learned not only all one ever learned of manual engineering, but also how to live as a man among men? The Lancashire workman was, and I suspect still is, a rough diamond. The genuine help and kindness which we all received was cloaked by a rugged exterior, a masterly understatement of life, and a deep hatred of ostentation and superficial 'show'.

This led to an unbreakable code of the ordinary which demanded cloth caps for the men, 'pot' hats for the foremen. This was a bit hard on a young man who had a train to catch straight from work, and who needed to be properly dressed to meet his girl friend. Any bowler or trilby hat smuggled in was quickly located and hoisted up to the rafters with the willing co-operation of the crane men. A clean sports jacket was lucky if it did not find itself bolted down to a bench in the corner of the shop, and if anyone tried to walk to work without his overalls on his life was soon made a burden to him. An old mate of mine in the millwright's shop used to be particularly scornful of men who had raised themselves or been raised off the shop floor, and who in consequence lost something of their old 'bonhomie' with former mates. "Look at him", he used to say, "walking about as if he had a waistcoat made out of his father's breeches' arse".

In such terms we received the salutary lesson very early in life not to get above ourselves, and however consumed with eagerness or bursting with pride internally, we learned to meet events with a proper scepticism and to comment upon them with the throw-away line.

Taking up again more personal matters the working day was followed on three nights a week by attendance at the Mechanics Institute from 7 to 9.30 p.m. with another evening devoted to homework. There a classical education was over laid by the essential elements of mechanical engineering. There also in the days before apprentice training schools with their directors and supervisors, lay the source of recognition and the gateway to preferment. Except for the full time principal, all of the teachers were amateurs, who by day held various jobs in local industry or on the Railway. The latter were able to spot young lads with the root of the matter in them, and in this way individuals were sometimes picked out for additional training.

Gass, the leading draughtsman referred to above, took the Machine Drawing Class, and it was not long before my plaguing him to know the why and wherefore led to visits to the Drawing Office to borrow books. This, together with the winning of a certain number of prizes for the different subjects, led to an interlude in my shop training. In February, 1919 soon after the end of the war, I left the stripping pit for a six month spell in the Drawing Office which eventually lasted 12 months. During this period I worked as already mentioned on production drawings for the rebuilding of the 4-cylinder 4–6–0's then in progress.

I suppose the really climacteric days of a lifetime can be counted on one's fingers. Humble stage in ambition as it now appears, that far off day of acceptance into the world of design was certainly one of mine. A drawing office is a workaday enough place, many of whose inmates spend much time scheming how to get out. What words however can describe the thrill of first entry, straight from the shops, and from the stripping pit at that, into a warm clean cloistered abode of shaded lights and quiet endeavour—that repository of design history and practice available for the mere opening of drawing cabinet or bookcase?

I must have done a fairly good job for when I returned to the shops in 1920 I pursued a special course under the Chief Draughtsman's patronage, covering new engine building in the erecting shop, motion fitting in the machine shop, a spell in the millwrights shop on works and outdoor machinery maintenance, finishing up with 6 weeks at Clifton Power Station, all this in conjunction with one day a week full time at Manchester College of Technology. On my 21st birthday my apprenticeship terminated with a return to the office as Draughtsman on the salaried staff at £240 per annum—a princely sum!

By this time the rebuilt 4–6–0's were fairly launched, No. 1522 being the first. New locomotives to the same design began coming out in August 1921 and eight were completed by the end of the year. Numerous Dynamometer Car tests took place mainly between Manchester and Blackpool, but a certain number were with heavy coal trains on the Yorkshire main line. Coming events were foreshadowed by a first test with No. 1519 between Crewe and Carlisle in December, while three test runs were made from Manchester to Blackpool with LNW engines. 'Prince of Wales' No. 1351 took 404 tons on Aug. 21st, 'Claughton' No. 192 took 394 tons on Oct. 9th and 474 tons on Oct. 30th.

The only other event of interest before the end of the Lancashire & Yorkshire railway was the dusting off of the old 2–10–0 project which had lurked in the background since the visit of officials to Belgium around 1911. Following study of the Flamme 4-cylinder 2–10–0's in that country, a 'Lanky' version had been schemed out at Horwich. The resurrection consisted of setting out the wheelbase and estimated weights on the Bridge Curve which produced an equivalent uniformly distributed bending moment from which the Civil Engineer's approval could be granted or withheld. It was withheld!

To round off this part of the story and to extend it a little into the area of the next chapter I recall the young men who were my contemporaries. We all shared lively hopes and fears regarding our progress, and many for one reason or another did not progress very far. Others left the service early, or were soon transferred to other departments, and were heard of no more.

Of others yet again who made a career on the railway I think of Eric Mason, already mentioned and destined to a motive power career and to authorship, and of Frank Horne, son of the Head Office Locomotive Inspector who is Chief Technical Assistant at Doncaster at this writing. Somewhat later came Fred Simpson from Barrow, to be eventually Works Manager of Derby Locomotive Works, and Fred Umpleby from Goole who ended up in charge of the Outdoor Machinery Department of the L.M. region at Derby. There was also 'Jimmy' Caldwell who became Mechanical Engineer (Design) at the same centre.

Of those who left I recollect Teddy Wade, nephew of Col. O'Brien, whom we envied in the relative freedom of pupilage, and Harry Fowler, son of the C.M.E. of the Midland Railway, talented as an amateur entertainer. Rob Kirkland, large in size and spirit was the nephew of Irwin, the Company's secretary, and after various posts on the workshop side he finished his engineering career in East Africa. There was Cyril Billington, son of the Chief Draughtsman, red haired, and more interested in girls than engines, who in due course departed to South America. Also Bill Selby, enthusiast for all things Great Western who soon entered the commercial world and who in the end retired from a senior position of the engineering staff of the Crown Agents.

The presence of these characters was part of the very texture of our young days at Horwich, and the mention of their names is not I think out of place in this evocation of a vanished age.

II

Amalgamation

1922-1925

ON Jan. 1st, 1922, the Lancashire & Yorkshire and London & North Western Railways were amalgamated, and some dubiety has existed ever since as to who took over who during the single year before the larger amalgamation which formed the L.M.S. From one point of view the L.N.W. was big, it had history and traditions on a grand scale, and lay second among main line companies in mileage. Moreover, it became known as Division A in the new concern while the L. & Y. was called Division B, and A is certainly ahead of B. On the other hand this juncture caught the L.N.W. at an awkward moment when some of its highest offices were vacant or newly filled so that L. & Y. men were appointed to certain key positions, including that of Chief Mechanical Engineer.

This circumstance faced technical development with some human problems from the very first day. To an extent only perhaps equalled at Swindon, Crewe had a tradition of veneration for the past and loyalty to an individual, so that when H. P. M. Beames, only appointed C.M.E. as recently as 1920, was rejected for the top engineering post in the new concern, and George Hughes was appointed in his stead, repercussions were set off which lasted for the next ten years.

The year of 1922 itself was a period of deceptive calm, in which a kind of phoney war was waged consisting of each side doing little more than getting the measure of the other. Each party continued to build to its own designs. Existing locomotives retained their old numbers, and liveries, and worked for the most part where they had worked before, although a few 'Princes' and 'Claughtons' found their way onto the L. & Y. for regular service and a little tentative running was done by Hughes rebuilt 4–6–0's on the West Coast main line. Little record remains however of these first interchanges.

There were soon comings and goings on the workshop side, and Lovatt Williams writing in the Railway Magazine in Mar./Apr.

Plate I. Group of current and former L. & Y. officers, 1912, with, below, a key.

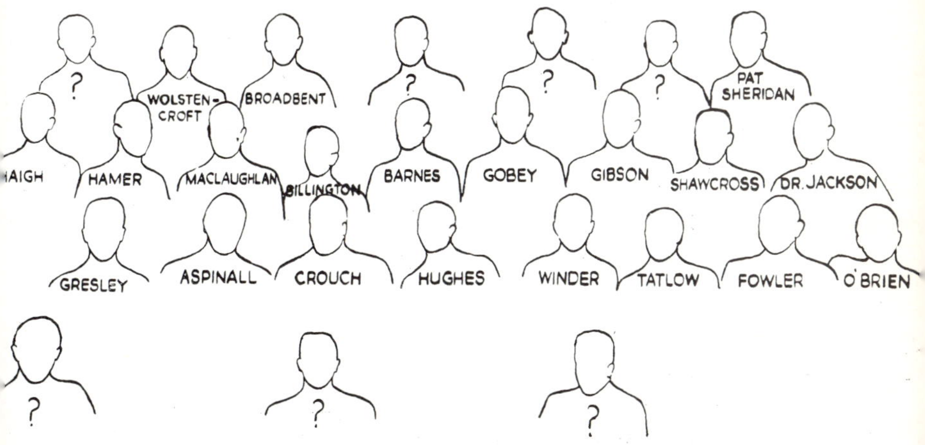

Plate 2. Horwich Works machine shop, 1917.

Plate 3. L. & Y. saturated large-boilered 0–8–0 No. 912, heads a westbound freight train near Kirkby.

Plate 4. L. & Y. 4–4–0 No. 1105, fitted with Schmidt superheater, heads a Manchester to Leeds express.

Plate 5. Original L. & Y. Atlantic No. 1400, as running in 1917, with a Manchester-York train.

Plate 6.
An Aspinall Atlantic, in original condition, on express duty.

Plate 7.
Hoy's 2–6–2T No. 387 in original condition.

Plate 8.
Hughes' saturated four-cylinder 4–6–0 No. 1518 leaves Manchester (Victoria) with the 5.0 p.m. Southport residential express.

1949 gave an amusing but realistic picture of some of these first contacts seen through the eyes of a Crewe man.[1]

On the design side there had immediately to be faced those questions which have remained with us ever since, through subsequent amalgamation culminating in British Railways. Questions affecting rolling stock policy such as :—Should one try to ascertain the best, in order to perpetuate it, to the exclusion of the less good, or ought one to accept without too much modesty that one's own previous practice must be the best and should therefore prevail? If the former, how is one to judge what is best, and if the latter, is one likely to prove strong enough to impose one's will rather than find acceptance by agreement? Yet again, would it be better to strike out into the blue without reference to what has gone before, be it good or bad?

Being a man with a logical mind Hughes set about trying to establish what was best between the rival locomotive designs within his new kingdom but he was quite without precedent as to how to go about it. He, therefore, instituted a process known as Co-ordination which in this first year took the rather peculiar form of patiently recording for Claughtons and L. & Y. 4–6–0's on the one hand, and for the most recent respective classes of 0–8–0's on the other, a vast mass of dimensional and statistical data, the compilation of which occupied much of my time in my first year as a draughtsman.

This brought about some visits to Crewe, and in this twilight before night descended upon old times and the sun rose upon the glories of the big amalgamation to be, we may turn aside for a moment to consider L.N.W.R. locomotives in their final pure form.

It has become the custom in much modern writing about the old companies to cast them in heroic mould, and to dwell upon their virtues in comparison with the industrial giants which superseded them. David is naturally favoured before Goliath and history does not record any shortcomings which the younger man may have had. Thus there is a whole literature about the good features of the better known North Western types. Precursors, Georges, Princes, Claughtons, with their simple design, their stout hearted performance, and the transformation they brought to West Coast running in the first stage as they replaced the old Webb Compounds, and, in the second stage, as in superheated form they broke all

[1] "Crewe Works and the L. & Y. Amalgamation"—Lovat Williams (*Railway Magazine*, Aug. 1960).

their own records. The story is well known and true, and all honour remains with those who designed, built and ran them. It is with no detriment to well established fact, therefore, that I now refer to certain shortcomings which leavened the whole. What I am about to say may shock those devotees of the 'Premier Line' who will ask how possibly could such failings be reconciled to the famous performance which has been so well authenticated. Nonetheless the shortcomings were facts no less than the performances, and the inter relation between the two will be enlarged upon presently. In part these troubles were the ailments of the time writ large; in part they were specialties of the Crewe tradition itself.

In common with the generality of practice piston valve heads were fitted with a single split cast iron ring, extending over the whole width. If suitably lubricated this was steam tight when new but, as ring and liner surfaces wore, the stiffness of the ring was incapable of following the new self-generated contour, and steam blow-by occurred which spoiled performance and could greatly increase coal consumption. As the onset and growth of this internal leakage, from the steam to the exhaust sides of the valve, was random it accounted for some of the poor performances which occasionally turned up.

Another cause of disappointing runs which afflicted the 4–6–0's, but not the 4–4–0's was the interference with free air flow through the fire-grate due to the firebox foundation ring being set too closely above the trailing or, in the case of the 'Prince of Wales' class, of the intermediate coupled axles. Not only did the humps in the ashpans where they passed over the axle interfere with air flow but ash, building up over the hump and in the shallow part of the pan, could accumulate to choke combustion air towards the end of a long run, so that the effective grate area was reduced. Once an engine could get into this kind of trouble at the back end, no amount of playing about with the blastpipe at the front end could get matters right. The Claughton in particular was prone to this failing.

Although not apparent to the onlooker inadequate bearings, poorly lubricated, were a prime cause of lack of availability and high maintenance costs.

Records show that in a given year, on a stock of 246 'Prince of Wales' engines there were 161 hot coupled axleboxes, of which 117 were on the leading driving axle, due to inadequate bearing surface to deal with the heavy piston thrust. On the Claughton the 4-cylinder arrangement neutralised the thrust, but a similar proportion of hot bearings occurred this time on the trailing axle-boxes. This was because the lubrication, originating from trimming type oil boxes above the footplate, was carried down through a steel pipe between trailing wheels and the frame, which entered an opening in the axlebox top. When heavy side wear occurred the trailing axleboxes moved far enough laterally to shear off the oil pipe end, with total loss of lubricant.

Although all this adds up for the two classes in question to only about one hot box per engine per annum, the cumulative effect in shed man hours, and in loss of use was considerable.

These kind of troubles were, as already stated, fairly common to all railways although the Crewe design did rather ask for more than its fair share due to the crudity of its design. There were, however, a number of other troubles in which the old L.N.W. were real specialists, in broken mainframes for example.

As they got older and the material became fatigued roughly half the total number of 'Prince of Wales' engines fractured their frames each year, usually adjacent to the leading driving horns, and the 'George V' class suffered similarly. Also a great deal of the detail work was shoddy, and splashers and cab sides rattled and loosened their attachments. The mortality of bearing springs was enormous, and injectors and their connections were unreliable and inaccessible.

A lot of this grief stemmed from a rather slavish following of the design ideas of Webb & Ramsbottom, and confirmation of what this meant even to the smaller locomotives was set out in a realistic account by J. M. Dunn in the Railway Magazine under the heading of 'L.N.W.R. Side Tank Coal Engines'.[1]

Although the old railway had run its trains and made money, taking all this trouble in its stride more or less as an Act of God, the new C.M.E. on his assumption of office, found himself faced with three further important troubles each calling for urgent action since safety was involved.

The first stemmed from a serious boiler explosion which occurred in 1921 at Buxton on 4-cylinder compound 0–8–0 coal engine No. 34. Although primarily due to a defective safety valve it drew attention to the very small volume available above the inner firebox for disengagement of steam, and the most numerous classes of L.N.W. engine were gradually fitted with Belpaire boilers from 1923 onwards as renewals were made.

[1] By J. M. Dunn (*Railway Magazine* Aug. 1960).

The second concerned Brake Power. A number of engine types were fitted with an economical idea by which a single brake cylinder under the cab applied both engine and tender brake blocks. How the L.N.W worked unfitted freight trains at all was something of a mystery. There is a record of some tests carried out on the L.Y.R. under equal conditions of load, running down a 1 in 100 gradient at a speed of 20 m.p.h. Horwich 0–8–0 No. 1369 stopped its train in 1,520 yards. From the same speed Crewe G2 class 0–8–0 No. 2182, also with vacuum brake on the engine, had accelerated to 22·5 m.p.h. after a distance of 3,860 yards under full brake application, and the train had to be brought to rest by the intervention of another locomotive inserted in the make up for just such an eventuality.

L.N.W. G1 class 0–8–0 No. 1585 with steam brake fared even worse. At the end of 3,055 yards under full braking, speed was 25 m.p.h., and there is a note on the test record that engine brakepower diminished when the driver blew the whistle, due no doubt to a common insufficient manifold supplying both!

After one or two run aways had occurred in service a widespread modification was introduced to fit separate brake cylinders on engine and tender and thus increase total brake power.

The third was an epidemic of broken connecting rods. In Joy's valve gear the whole of the valve motion is derived fron a pin threaded through the main body of the connecting rod about a third of the way along from the little end. This always a point of weakness, on the L. & Y. taking the form of fracture of the pin, which promptly decanted the whole of the valve gear downward onto the track—the 'Dropped Motion' of many urgent telegrams. On the L.N.W.R. under possibly more onerous running conditions it was the connecting rods themselves which flawed and broke, and there were several nasty cases in the years just after the war. One solution was to design a stronger connecting rod, on which I spent an interesting summer month in 1923. The other was to develop an outside Walschaert gear driving the inside valves through rocking shafts. This was done at Crewe, and four 'Prince of Wales' were thus fitted—the well known 'Tishy's' (Plate 12). Since the trouble died down with the infiltration of the new rods the greater expense of the outside valve gear could no longer be justified.

Now the defects which I have enumerated were all facts, but their effect upon the locomotives varied with time and with standards of maintenance. Before 1917 coal and labour were cheap, so that deterioration in efficiency and the need for high man hours to keep the engine on the road were not so seriously considered as they are today. Thus more frequent piston ring and liner changes, meticulous care of the lubrication system, painstaking cleaning of ashpan and the early tightening up of everything that was loose undoubtedly went a long way to secure a reasonable level of reliability. Once this care was relaxed, first in the war years, and then in all the uncertainty after the war, design weaknesses, hitherto held in check, claimed their toll. Once labour became scarce or dear in relation to former times then the noonday of locomotive nursing on the maintenance side was over, and what formerly sufficed became inadequate.

Matters were aggravated, first by the tradition dating from Moon and Webb, that locomotives must be very cheap in initial cost. Secondly when the new wine of larger cylinders and superheated steam was poured into the old bottles of the 'Precursor' and 'Experiment' classes, for example, the heavy thrusts which produced the wonderful performances simply broke up axleboxes and frames which had become inadequate to the task.

Finally the superb performances could only have been achieved by those of the top link engines, on which either the various deteriorations mentioned above had not begun to act, or were mitigated by the provision of generous maintenance attention. It was hardly worth the effort of even the most enthusiastic train timers to record the runs made by the others!

Much of this continuance of old design practice was undoubtedly due to two men who ended their long careers at about this time. Jackson, the Chief Draughtsman, retired at the end of 1920, and Sackfield, Leading Draughtsman, in August 1923. The latter had served the L.N.W.R. for 51 years. Both had in their most formative years survived the autocratic régime of Francis Webb. The iron had clearly eaten into their souls and it was not for them to question the laws which had been handed down on tablets of stone. Grover, the new Chief Draughtsman, a much more forward looking engineer had, like his new chief at Crewe, only a single year in which to act independently. Thereafter, until he retired in his turn in 1940, he had to work under the shadow first of Horwich and later of Derby. As he had to serve as the channel through which alien ideas from the latter centres reached his master, Beames, I fear he had more than a few unhappy times.

Reverting to 1922, the year of the greater L.N.W.R., apart from the co-ordination documentation already referred to, design activity at Crewe was confined to completion of the drawings for a new series of 0–8–4 tank engines turned out in 1923—pure L.N.W. design based upon their standard coal engines. This engine was also very painful to maintain, and Dunn has described what it meant to the shed staff in South Wales area in which it worked.[1]

The only other requirement thrown up from the operating side during this year was the need for a more powerful tank engine for use over the whole line, and a total of 60 units were talked about at first. Without hesitation Hughes decided that this should be based upon his rebuilt 4–6–0 of which more new ones had just been ordered, and a 4–6–4 wheel arrangement was the natural result. After juggling on the Bridge Curve with wheel spacings and water and coal capacity the Horwich office was set to work on production drawings of a locomotive, the boiler and forward part of which was identical with the 4–6–0's except for a longer wheelbase bogie. Short sidetanks, and a deep bunker resting on a duplicate bogie made up the rear part of the design. In the outcome an order was given for 30, but in the last resort only 10 were turned out as tank engines in 1924 (Plate 13), the remaining 20 appearing as tender engines in that and the following year. It is clear that the restricted route availability of this massive engine was the cause of the shrinkage in the initial demand.

Nobody has come forward to chronicle what occurred at managerial level in this experimental year. It to be assumed that for most of it the lengthening shadow of the impending larger grouping gradually suspended individual action.

On January 1st, 1923, the London Midland & Scottish Railway came into being with 10,316 steam locomotives of 393 different types, a few of the lesser known of which are illustrated in Plates 14, 15, 16 & 17. George Hughes was again appointed Chief Mechanical Engineer and he chose to retain his technical headquarters at Horwich, much to the disgust of visitors' and firms' representatives who had to struggle in the branch line trains and in tramcars to reach the new but remote seat of power. Sir Henry Fowler of the Midland became Deputy C.M.E., and four others, Beames of the L.N.W., Hookham of the North Stafford, Pickersgill of the Caledonian and Whitelegg of the G. & S. W. survived as Mechanical Engineers in their former provinces but shorn of any independent responsibility for rolling stock design.

A big administrative change with large repercussions upon future locomotive design was the separation in the new group of

[1] "Memories of the L.N.W. 0–8–4 Tank Engines"—J. M. Dunn (*Railway Magazine* April 1953).

motive power from the functions of the C.M.E., following Midland rather than L.N.W. and L. & Y. former practice. The new Motive Power Department, located at Derby, was nominally jointly responsible to the C.M.E and the Chief Operating Officer. J. E. Anderson, however, now in charge, viewed all locomotive requirements as they arose in terms of Midland thinking, powerfully backed by J. H. Follows who became Vice President in charge of operations. Henceforth for a number of years it was to be the operators who called the tune culminating in a dramatic duality in the formation of design policy which will be presently described.

Of the physical position at Grouping I cannot do better than quote what I have previously written in a paper to the Institution of Locomotive Engineers.[1]

" High degree superheating had been accepted for all important new construction since 1910 and numerous existing engines had been converted. In all 1,882 superheated engines existed. In addition to forty-five 4–4–0 express engines on the Midland, compounding was represented by eleven 0–8–0 freight engines on the L.Y.R., and ninety-eight Webb survivals on the L.N.W.R., of 4–4–0, 0–8–0 and 2–8–0 types. Stephenson's valve gear was the most widely used, but Joy's gear on the L.N.W. and L.Y.R. sections ran it a close second. Two hundred and twenty-three engines had Walschaert Gear. Valve travel of 4″ to 4½″ and steam lap of about 1″ was all but universal. Only 33 engines had valve travel over 6″, and of these only four had as much as 1½″ lap (actually only one of these latter survived at January 1st, 1923).

" Restrictions in weight per foot run were especially severe on the Midland while the loading gauge, except on the Caledonian, allowed only a limited width at platform level, one reason for the small number of outside cylinder types. On the other hand any engine for general use north of the border, apart from the main line between Carlisle and Glasgow, had to be restricted to a height of 12′ 11″ although 13′ 5½″ was permissible on the L.Y.R. The L.N.W. and L. & Y. main lines were equipped with water troughs roughly every 30 miles and thus required only small tenders. Midland troughs were spaced every 50 miles and Scotland had no troughs at all.

" Each company believed the engine types it had developed were especially suited to the natural features of its own lines and traffic conditions. Until the preliminary amalgamation of the L.N.W.R.

[1] " A Modern Locomotive History "—E. S. Cox (*Proceedings*, Inst. Loco. Engs. No. 190, 1964).

and L.Y.R. in 1922 hardly any exchange of locomotives between one company and another had taken place within the lines forming the L.M.S., nor was there much interchange of design data.

"In general the best performances in efficiency and reliability came from the smaller, older types which carried superheaters. With few exceptions the larger and later classes were less satisfactory. The newly formed group lacked a first class modern express locomotive for the heavy Anglo-Scottish trains, a mixed traffic type of wide range, a large general purpose passenger tank, and a large main line freight engine."

As will be described later, design work upon all of these requirements was put in hand over the ensuing few years, but some of the immediate effects of the amalgamation may be referred to first.

The expected locomotive renumbering and the associated new livery arrived together in the second half of 1923. Midland red was by far the most attractive colour used by the old companies, and Midland influence, to become paramount before long, had already sufficient power to ensure its adoption. In the renumbering, Midland numbers remained, L.N.W. started in the 5000's and L. & Y. with No. 10000 which was bestowed upon Hughes' private saloon equipment with its Ramsbottom designed 2–4–0. Scottish engines began at 14000 and all locomotives carried, to begin with, the large numerals on tender or tank sides, previously used by the Midland. No. 10447 was the first new Hughes engine to be painted in this way with a 7′ 3″ 4–4–0 as the first repainted engine. We gazed in wonder at these phenomena, positively gaudy after the long régime of black. The cast iron number plates on the smoke box door were a great blessing since it had been impossible previously to find out the engine number from the front.

Midland Red turned out to be something like Caledonian Blue, all things to all men! It soon became apparent that L. & Y. 'red' was several shades darker than the home product while the Scottish version only just managed to be red at all. Also while the other constituents seemed resigned to banishing the old colours from their paint shops, Crewe found an opportunity to express its extreme distaste for the whole procedure, and very few indeed of its locomotives were turned out in the hated apparel—its stocks of black paint seemed inexhaustable!

Still pursuing his policy of trying to determine and use the best, Hughes now gave the co-ordination work a more realistic turn by setting up a new committee and calling upon it to examine the principal fittings and components and to recommend which should be adopted as standard. The main committee consisted of the ex-C.M.E.'s, while the devilling was done by the Chief Draughtsmen and their staffs. Fusible plugs, boiler fittings, piston rings, tyres and whistles were treated, until the weight of new construction swung decisively towards Midland types, and eventual Midlandisation. As Lovatt Williams has mentioned this period gave rise to the first whistle concert—the second and last took place 30 years later as will be seen when British Railways standard locomotives are referred to.

One whistle from each former company was mounted upon a long steampipe fed by the works boiler and the idea was to stand a long way off out on the Horwich 'Moss', probably the bleakest place in Lancashire, and to judge which was the most pleasing. The actual concert occurred on December 18th, 1923, and I don't think any of the ex-C.M.E.'s, assembled for the purpose, thought much of the whole proceedings. I saw them as they returned to the offices, and since the display had proved largely abortive anyway due to low steam pressure and condensation, their cup of misery was full. It was a historic moment, for the ranks were soon to thin out, and I think of tubby Henry Fowler with the points to his moustache, and Beames with his habitual expression of having swallowed something disagreeable—on this day tremendously accentuated—Pickersgill with his white quiff of hair, Whitelegg tall and angular, and Hookham with his large head. Even if there was no man of great stature among them, they all nevertheless had run their former departments with greater power and responsibility than more modern conditions have permitted to those who followed them, and all honour is due to their memory as inheritors of traditions long vanished.

To finish the whistle story, the melodious Caledonian siren was judged the most acceptable, and one was fitted for trial to an L. & Y. 'Atlantic'. Unfortunately it was heard one day in Manchester Victoria by the Follows/Anderson part of the locomotive Axis, which had been no party to the concert or its results. Orders went out for its immediate removal, and ten years were to elapse before its reappearance as the sign-audible of an altogether different régime.

O'Brien, having been appointed Electrical Engineer, began at once to build up a new staff at Horwich, and at the very beginning of 1923 became occupied with proposals to electrify the Crewe-Carlisle section of the West Coast main line. As early as the end of January I was set to work upon diagrams for a possible 2–D–2 electric locomotive for this service.

This was rather naturally based upon Swiss practice since the Swiss were pioneering in electric locomotive design at this time, and to obtain first hand data for its further development two special Dynamometer car tests were made over the proposed route. The first was on June 24th when Hughes rebuilt 4–6–0's, Nos. 1511 and 1658, worked a 500 ton train. This run, on which I assisted by pressing a bell push on the leading engine to record on the chart each shovelful of coal, was attended by a large bevy of top brass. A somewhat indifferent performance on the part of the two engines rather marred the proceedings, and a photograph which was taken at Carlisle on arrival shows a distinctly overheated smokebox door! The second run was made on November 18th in the same year with Nos. 1669 and 1670 hauling 640 tons. This time, the record states, the run was satisfactory.

The results of these tests, and a great deal of other preparatory work, were duly incorporated in a paper which O'Brien read to the Institution of Electrical Engineers in 1924.[1] This brought nemesis in its wake for the newly formed management at Euston was by no means prepared to embark at once upon schemes of such magnitude. Acute differences of opinion must have arisen for O'Brien promptly resigned and retired to Ireland. His newly formed department was quickly disbanded and its elements became absorbed into the less enterprising Euston office of Cortez-Leigh, of the former L.N.W., who thenceforth reigned in his stead.

Billington, promoted Technical Assistant to the C.M.E. in April, used three members of the Drawing Office to undertake what would today be the work of a Development section, namely to cover all the technical investigation, forward scheming and relations with other departments which the large combine demanded to an extent scarcely felt on the old compact L. & Y. In this trio, consisting of Frank Stubbs, Arthur Phillips and myself, my job was mainly concerned with the new locomotive projects. This consisted of preparing a diagram for each proposal, with estimated axle weights, usually to a scale of ½" to the foot. Also a cross section of front and rear, at 1½" to the foot, on which the throwover on curves was marked in relation to the loading gauge, and the setting out of two locomotives plus heavy wagons on the Bridge Curve. This latter was a graphical means of establishing the equivalent uniform distributed bending load per foot run appropriate to bridge spans from 10 to 160 feet.

[1] "The Future of Main Line Electrification on British Railways"—H. E. O'Brien (*Proceedings* Inst. Electrical Engrs. 1924).

In those days the Civil Engineers would release no information on the criteria by which the acceptability or otherwise of any given locomotive for the various routes was decided. Thus all the design office could do was to set out its new proposal on the Bridge Curve in comparison with some existing locomotive which was already allowed to run over the desired routes. If the new locomotive exceeded the load diagram for the old, there was no guidance as there is now as to how much excess was acceptable or what changes the Civil Engineers required. Designs were simply accepted or rejected out of hand.

This was a supremely time-wasting exercise for it meant that the whole process had to be gone through again and again (eight times in the case of the Baltic Tank, for example), until Olympian acquiescence was won. Similarly with throwover on curves—there might only be one or two bridges or platforms on a 300-mile route which prevented passage, but it was unthinkable that these might be rebuilt. It was not until Stanier's advent that a more realistic and compliant attitude was forthcoming, but that is another story.

When the operating needs and the Civil Engineers' reactions are met a steam locomotive outline is almost self-generating. However, notwithstanding my junior position I was able to influence to a considerable extent the appearance of the various projects as they emerged, a matter in which I took an intense interest. It is strange that so few of the locomotive engineers with whom I have worked have had any strong views as to what a locomotive should look like. They might know exactly what they want it to consist of but, for the most part, were only too glad to find someone with enough idea to get it down in clear diagram form.

By the end of 1923 there had only been slight stirrings but thereafter, until Hughes' retirement in 1925, active work proceeded on a 2–6–0, a 4–6–2 and corresponding 2–8–2, and a Garratt, the development of each of these I now propose to describe.

Among the very few new projects discovered in the various design offices when they were taken over was a proposal for a large mixed traffic 2–6–0 worked out in some detail at St. Rollox. This engine, which carried features common with the Caledonian '60' and ex Highland 'River' classes, had large horizontal outside cylinders which ruled it out at once for use on any of the English lines. A fresh start was therefore made at Horwich and many versions were offered before the design was finally frozen for production. They are listed in Table 1 and diagrams of some of them are shown in Figs. 1, 2, 3 & 4.

Table I. Development of Horwich 2–6–0 (1924-1926)

Scheme No.	*Horwich Drawing No.*	*Date*	*Wheel Arrange-ment*	*Cylinders Dia. × Stroke*	*Coupled Wheels Dia.*	*Boiler Pressure lbs./sq. in.*	*Tractive Effort lbs.*	*Maximum Axle Weight* T. C.	*Total Engine Weight* T. C.	*Comments*	*Fig. No. in text*
1	—	1923	2–6–0	21″ × 28″	5′ 6″	180	28624	20. 0	72. 0	Caledonian proposal	—
2	16909	2/24	2–6–0	20½″ × 26″	5′ 6″	180	25950	18. 0	62. 0	Midland Compound boiler	—
3	16919	2/24	2–6–0	21″ × 28″	5′ 6″	180	29280	19. 0	66. 0	' Prince of Wales ' boiler	1
4	—*	4/24	4–6–0	21″ × 28″	6′ 6″	180	24200	18. 0	74. 0	4–6–0 version of above	—
5	—*	4/24	2–6–4T	21″ × 28″	5′ 6″	180	29280	19. 0	90. 0	Tank engine version of 3 above	—
6	17080	5/24	2–6–0	21″ × 28″	5′ 6″	180	29280	19. 0	66. 0	New boiler	2
7	17338	7/24	2–6–0	21″ × 28″	5′ 6″	180	29280	19. 0	68. 0	' Baltic ' Tank boiler	3
8	17604	11/24	2–6–0	21″ × 28″	5′ 6″	180	29280	18.18	66. 4	Final scheme L. & Y. details	—
9	17619	11/24	2–6–0	20½″ × 26″	5′ 6″	180	25350	17.10	59. 0	Reduced weight Midland G8S boiler†	4
10	17632	11/24	2–6–0	21″ × 26″	5′ 6″	180	26580	18.10	65.10	As 8 above. Shorter firebox and wheelbase	—
11	17641	11/24	2–6–0	21″ × 26″	5′ 6″	180	26580	18.10	65.10	Final scheme as 8 above. Midland details	—
		1926	2–6–0	21″ × 26″	5′ 6″	180	26580	19.12	66. 0	As built	Plate 18

* Unnumbered diagrams.

† As used on Midland Class 3 4–4–0 (700 Class).

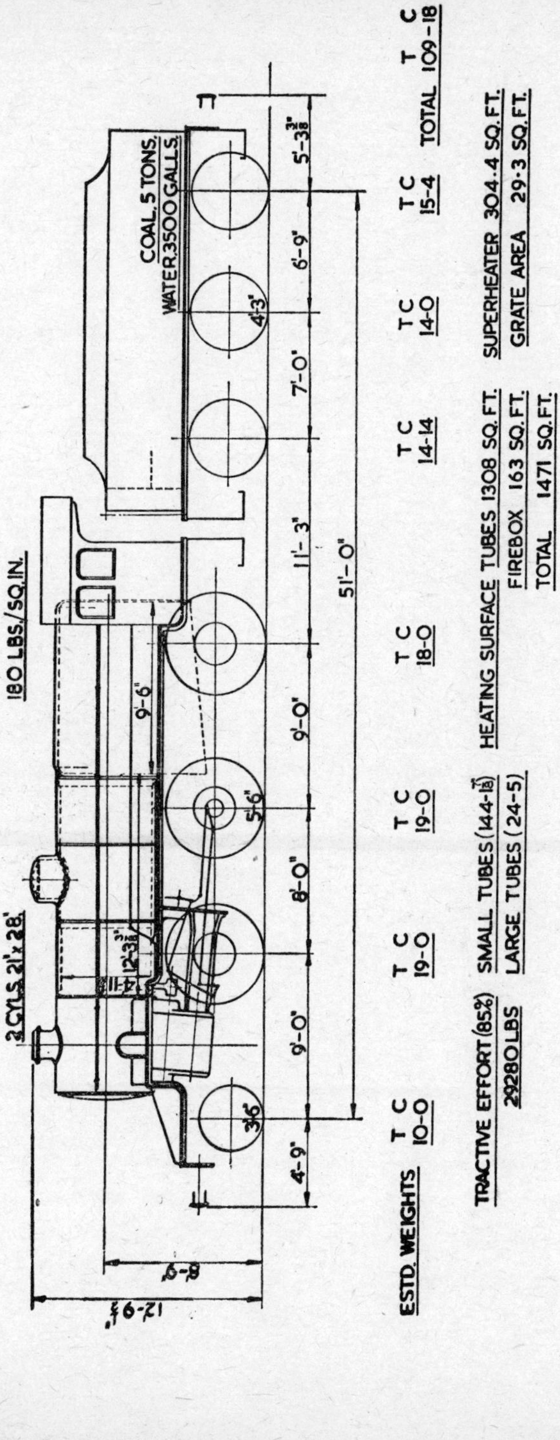

PROPOSED 2-6-0 WITH MODIFIED CREWE "PRINCE OF WALES" BELPAIRE BOILER.

Fig. 1

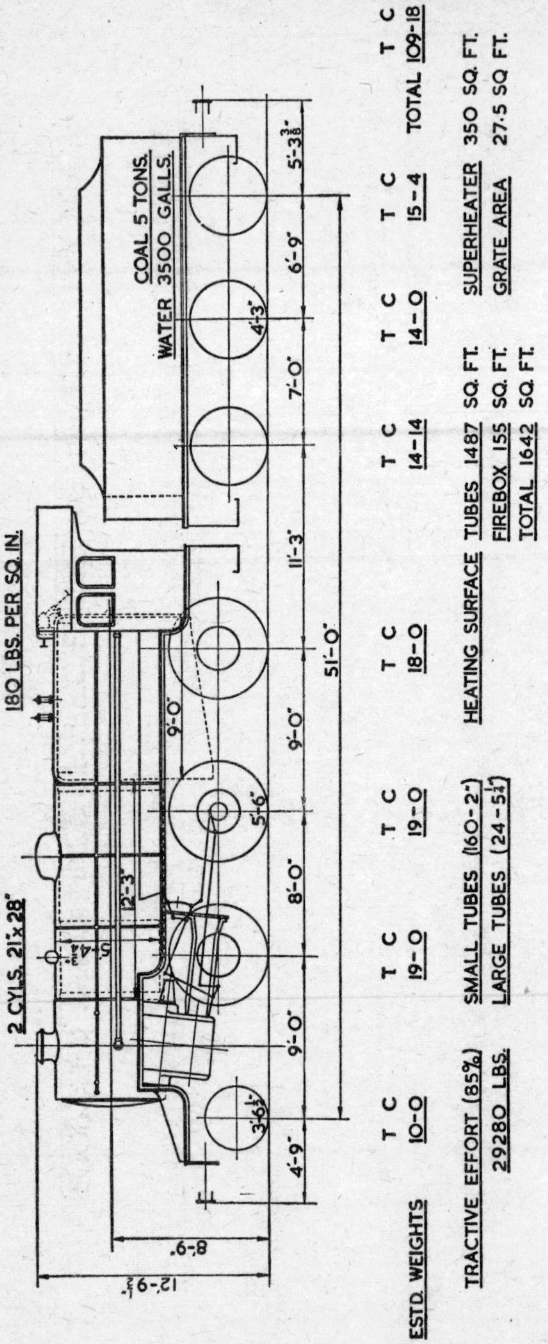

PROPOSED 2-6-0 MIXED TRAFFIC ENGINE.

Fig. 2

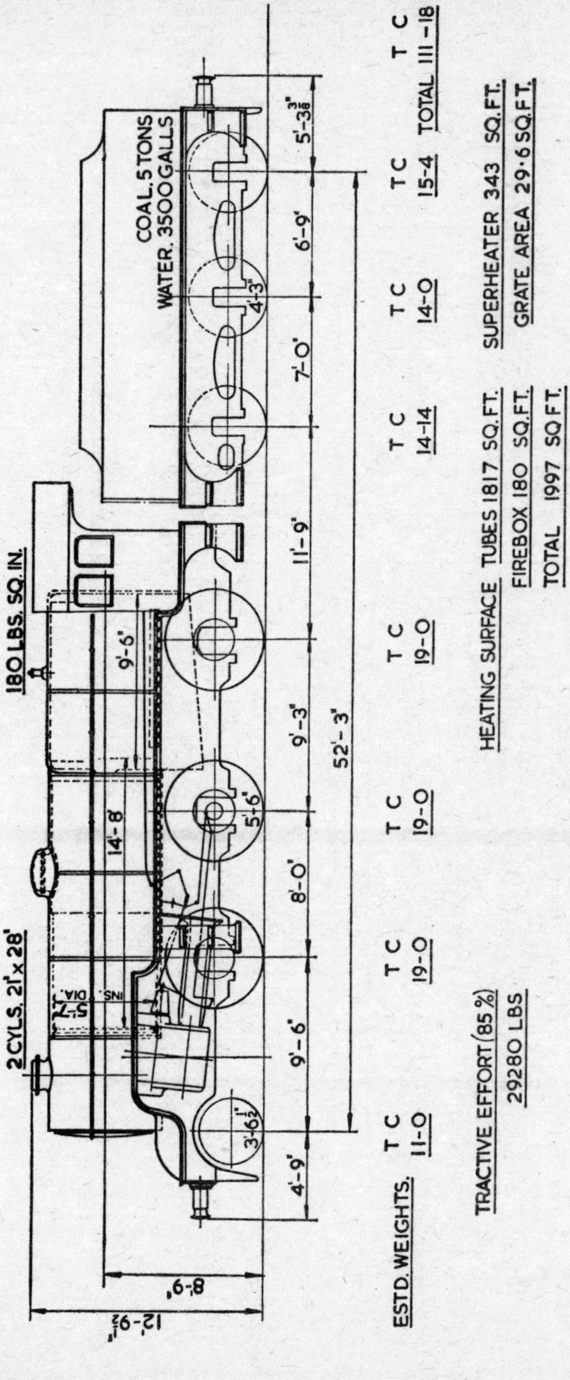

PROPOSED 2-6-0 MIXED TRAFFIC ENGINE WITH BALTIC TANK BOILER.

Fig. 3

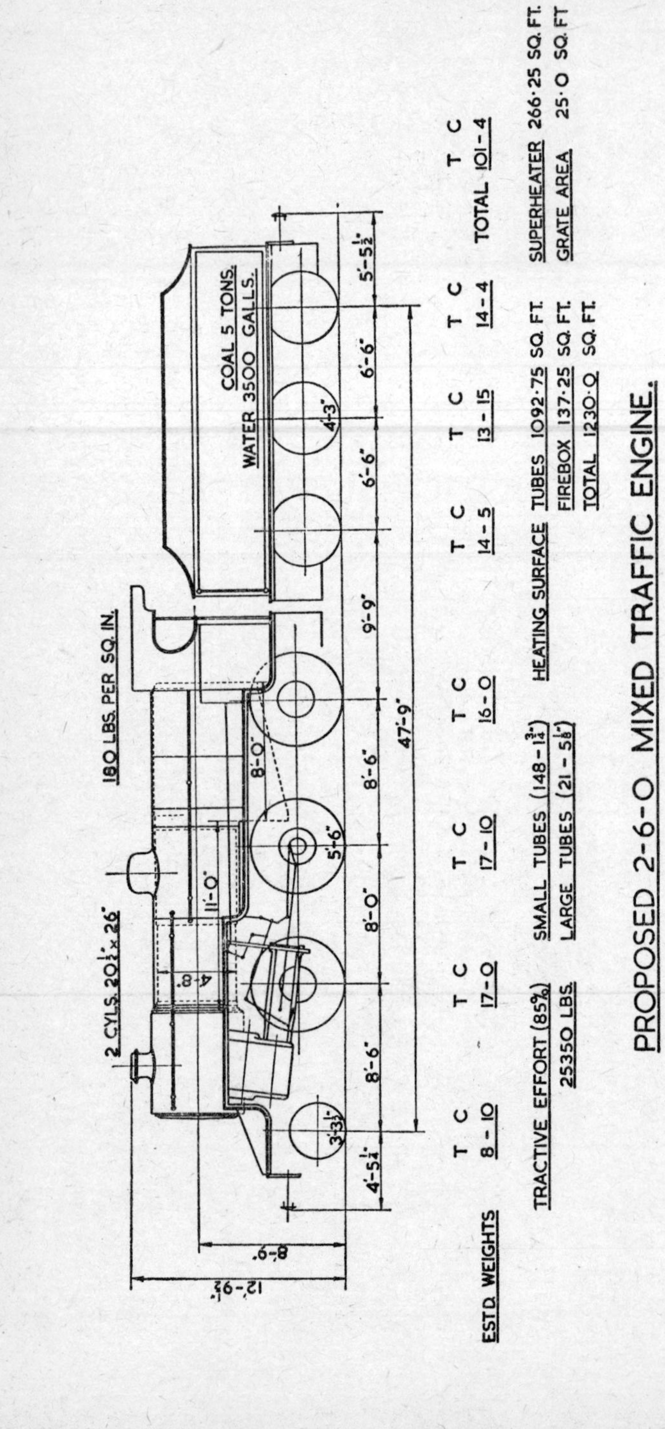
PROPOSED 2-6-0 MIXED TRAFFIC ENGINE.
2 CYLS. 20½" x 26"
180 LBS. PER SQ. IN.
COAL 5 TONS.
WATER 3500 GALLS.
12'-9½"
8'-9"
4'-8"
11'-0"
8'-0"
3'-3½"
5'-6"
4'-3"
4'-5¼"
8'-6"
8'-0"
8'-6"
9'-9"
6'-6"
6'-6"
5'-5½"
47'-9"
ESTD. WEIGHTS
T C 8 - 10
T C 17 - 0
T C 17 - 10
T C 16 - 0
T C 14 - 5
T C 13 - 15
T C 14 - 4
T C TOTAL 101 - 4
TRACTIVE EFFORT (85%) 25350 LBS.
SMALL TUBES (148 - 1¾")
LARGE TUBES (21 - 5⅛")
HEATING SURFACE TUBES 1092·75 SQ. FT.
FIREBOX 137·25 SQ. FT.
TOTAL 1230·0 SQ. FT.
SUPERHEATER 266·25 SQ. FT.
GRATE AREA 25·0 SQ. FT.

Fig. 4

Plate 9. Cab view of L. & Y. Atlantic No. 702.

Plate 10. L. & Y. four-car electric set as running in 1917, on the Liverpool-Southport Line. The end motor cars are of the original 1904 pattern, modified. The trailers are later elliptical-roof vehicles.

Plate 11. Interior view of third-class saloon of the L. & Y. 10 ft. wide Southport stock.

Plate 12. L.N.W. 'Prince of Wales' 4–6–0 No. 5845 *Prince of Wales* built with outside Walschaerts valve gear, and seen here in L.M.S. crimson lake livery.

Plate 13. Hughes' four-cylinder 4–6–4T No. 11115.

Plate 14. Wirral Railway 4–4–4T No. 14 heads a Seacombe-West Kirby train.

Plate 15. North Staffordshire Railway 0–6–2T No. 157 approaching Stoke with a train of L.N.W. coaches.

In the first phase, ending in May 1924, a new boiler was proposed in conjunction with cylinders of moderate inclination. These latter were each to be cast with half the smokebox saddle as in American practice. Also a steam manifold, 'drowned' injectors and top-feed represented new thinking for Horwich. In the last phase, before Derby took over, the cylinders were more steeply inclined, involving a very high running plate at the front end, for the sake of greater route availability. This was necessitated by the 21″ diameter cylinders which had to be used due to Hughes' unshakeable determination not to use any boiler-pressure higher than 180 lbs. to the sq. in.

The cylinders and valve gear were entirely new. Their design followed a most intensive study of recent American practice as described in certain currently available publications.[1,2] Piston valves of 11″ diameter were selected of hollow trunk type, without pressure release valves, and the thick stiff piston rings of previous Horwich practice were replaced by much more flexible rings of smaller cross section. $1\frac{1}{2}''$ steam lap was selected in conjunction with a $6\frac{3}{8}''$ valve travel. The Walschaert gear was extremely robust and was largely based upon Pennsylvania Railroad layout and details. The whole of the foregoing, owing nothing to former L. & Y. practice, gave effective, accurate, and readily maintainable steam distribution. For the first time on the L.M.S. a modern standard of performance and efficiency was maintained. This achievement was greatly strengthened by the substantial coupled axleboxes which were also provided.

A minor tragedy occurred in the model engineering world when a well-known firm, anxious to be first in the field, went to town on a mass-produced series of 'O' gauge locomotives based upon the phase one diagram. By the time the model was ready for marketing the appearance of the full-scale locomotive had changed considerably, and it must have puzzled model railway enthusiasts for many years afterwards why the model which they could buy was so unlike the real thing.

The first locomotive was turned out in 1926 and its advent at Derby, home of prim inside cylinder engines and low footplates, was as shocking as that of a striptease girl at a meeting of Plymouth Brethren would have been. But the new creation soon established its solid worth, not only at home in Lancashire, but also over the

[1] *Locomotive Valves and Valve Gears*—Yoder and Wharen (Van Nostrand, New York, 1917).

[2] *Modern Locomotive Valves and Valve Gears*—McShane (Griffiths & Winters, Chicago, 1918).

length of the ex-L.N.W. and even of the Midland, where nothing so eminently suitable for heavy fast freight had hitherto appeared (Plate 18). In all 245 were built and distributed all over the system. Ten of them were even drafted onto the Highland to help out the hard-pressed ' Clans '.

The need for a more powerful express passenger engine for the West Coast main line was self-evident. The former L.N.W. engines, badly run down during the war, were suffering from the various disabilities already described, and could only be brought to work the still rather easy schedules by dint of much double-heading and special means of identifying units which were in a reasonable state of repair. It was natural that the appearance of Gresley's first ' Pacific ' in 1922, closely followed by Raven's version on the N.E.R., should turn the C.M.E.'s mind towards something similar for the L.M.S. As a result early in 1923 a tentative diagram was produced and some calculations made as to possible performances. Thereafter a long silence followed, and it presently became apparent that a quite different solution was being contemplated in the South. The Midland had always followed a policy of small engines and light train loads, its whole passenger philosophy being based upon ' little and often '. The new operating heirachy therefore visualised splitting up the West Coast services into separate portions, each capable of being worked by a Midland type 4–4–0 compound. Large new orders were proposed for these which were in fact turned out from 1924 onwards. The traffic did not however prove amenable to this treatment. When eventually the new Royal Scot service was introduced in 1927 two compounds were required for the Glasgow to Carnforth section, and a ' Claughton ' and a ' George ' thence to Euston. So the position was not in fact solved by the proposed means, and the need for a large locomotive was just as acute in 1927 as it was in 1923. On the other hand, as a result of this five years' delay, an infinitely better product was obtained in the form of the eventual ' Royal Scot ' than would have been the case had any of the intervening Pacific ideas matured. Reasons for this will become clear in due course.

It was due to the growing interest in a heavy freight engine for the Toton to Brent coal traffic that the next step towards a ' Pacific ' was taken. It seemed sensible to develop the 2–8–2, which was the current thinking for the freight job, side by side with the passenger engine in order that a common boiler and other components could be worked out for both. In June 1924 a serious proposal was submitted, the 4–6–2 taking the form shown in Fig. 5.

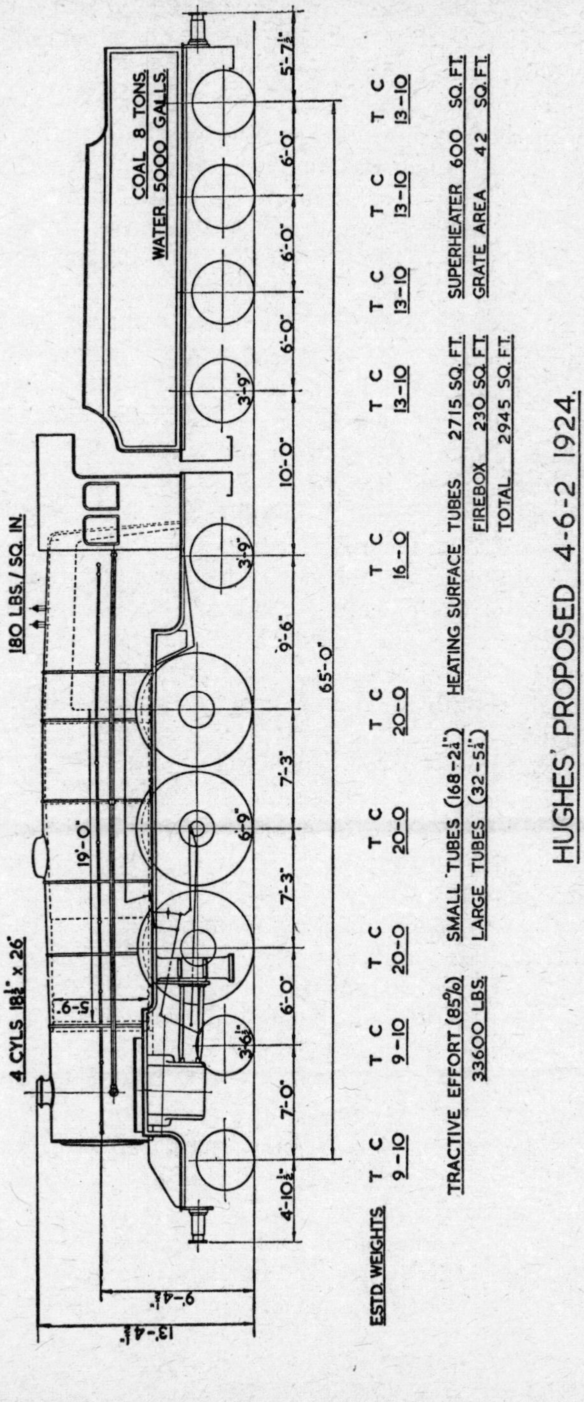
4 CYLS 18½" x 26"
180 LBS./SQ. IN.
19'-0"
5'-9"
9'-4½"
13'-4½"
COAL 8 TONS
WATER 5000 GALLS.
3'-6½"
6'-9"
3'-9"
3'-9"
4'-10½"
7'-0"
6'-0"
7'-3"
7'-3"
9'-6"
10'-0"
6'-0"
6'-0"
6'-0"
5'-7½"
65'-0"
ESTD. WEIGHTS
T C 9-10
T C 9-10
T C 20-0
T C 20-0
T C 20-0
T C 16-0
T C 13-10
T C 13-10
T C 13-10
T C 13-10
TRACTIVE EFFORT (85%) 33600 LBS.
SMALL TUBES (168-2¼")
LARGE TUBES (32-5¼")
HEATING SURFACE TUBES 2715 SQ. FT.
FIREBOX 230 SQ. FT.
TOTAL 2945 SQ. FT.
SUPERHEATER 600 SQ. FT.
GRATE AREA 42 SQ. FT.
HUGHES' PROPOSED 4-6-2 1924.

Fig. 5

The centrepiece of this exercise was to use 4 cylinders and 2 sets of valve gear following the design of the rebuilt Hughes 4–6–0 as closely as possible. By the end of the year the 2–8–2, having changed to a 3-cylinder proposal, necessitated the 4–6–2 diagram being altered accordingly, but no work was done on scheming the arrangement in any detail. That was the end of the Hughes' 'Pacific', the next move which turned it into a 4-cylinder compound only coming after his retirement, and thus belonging to the next chapter.

As distinct from its passenger services the Midland could not, for line occupation reasons, deal with its heavy Toton to Brent coal traffic in other than large train loads. This called for two 0–6–0's with a footplate crew of four as a permanent arrangement on each train (Plate 19). Thus, from the very beginning, there was considerable activity in seeking a single large engine design, but this was far from easy due to the severe dimensional and axleweight limitations which existed.

Two solutions were pursued in parallel, a 2–8–2 and a Garratt. At first there were some tentative ideas of 2–6–2's and 2–8–2's with booster on the trailing axle, this device having come into vogue in the U.S.A. as a means of getting more low speed tractive effort. However, the more definite proposal of mid-1924 consisted of a straightforward 2–8–2 having 4 cylinders and a wide firebox boiler interchangeable with the projected 4–6–2. As distinct from the latter, Anderson was taking a real interest in the freight proposal, and he pressed strongly for 3 rather than 4 cylinders. This was accepted and in the early part of 1925 quite serious work was undertaken in the Horwich office in working out cylinder, valve gear details and the design concept as a whole. Immediately upon Hughes' retirement this work was stopped and thereafter the 2–8–2, like the Pacific, was redeveloped as a compound.

Because of the great difficulty of getting the 2–8–2 inside the Midland Bridge Curve, at any practical axle weight, there was naturally much interest in articulated proposals which would spread the weight over a much longer locomotive wheelbase. In 1923 the Garratt was very much in its infancy, but Mallet type locomotives were well established in America and in certain overseas countries. A 0–6–6–0 Mallet scheme was therefore examined but since it gave so unfavourable a loading effect on the Bridge Curve for equal axle weights compared with the Garratt, it was promptly rejected. With a 2–6–0, 0–6–2 arrangement in mind Hughes now approached Beyer Peacock's in March 1925 who finally recommended a 2–6–2, 2–6–2 scheme. This design, had it been accepted. would have been a largely Beyer Peacock product in which cylinders, valve gear and bearing dimensions would have followed their own practice and experience. Estimates were called for and there the matter rested so far as Hughes and Horwich were concerned. For proposals from rival firms in the form of Kitson-Meyer, and 'North British modified Fairlie' articulated machines were examined but rejected as much inferior in one respect or another compared with the Garratt.

While all of the foregoing development work was going on, accompanied by a good deal of frustration, the existing Hughes 4-cylinder 4–6–0 which could have provided the temporary salvation of the West Coast line failed to do so. Batches of these engines were built new and drafted to the ex-L.N.W., but they did not show any great advantage over the Claughtons in that territory, any more than they did in Dynamometer car trials of the two engines carried out over the Manchester-Blackpool main line. In sheer pulling power the Horwich products could always win at the lower speeds, but in sustained high speed running they fell short. It was for this reason that their use was largely confined to working north of Crewe, while their forays down to Euston were few and far between (Plate 20). Notwithstanding their apparently good valve proportions and events they were not very economical, and their sustained steaming was uncertain on the long haul.

Moreover their record in hot bearings, once away from the short runs of the L. & Y., was anything but good, the imperfectly sealed oil wells cast in the top of the axleboxes forming the sole, and inadequate, means of lubrication. It is clear now that the type of thick piston ring employed, plus early deterioration in the ball pressure release valves with which the valve heads were fitted, caused epidemic steam leakage past the valves which impaired both performances and economy. Meanwhile the built-up smokebox and the arrangement of exhaust connections could impair steaming by permitting entry of air at the front end to spoil the draught.

With no realisation of what was really at fault a good deal of work went on, with which I was associated in early 1924, in increasing the steam lap and playing about with the lead. Eliptical valve event diagrams showed the possibility of marked improvement by adjusting these values. Engine 1656 was the guinea pig, and within the existing valve travel of $6\frac{3}{8}''$ an eventual optimum combination of $1\frac{7}{16}''$ lap and $\frac{1}{4}''$ lead was arrived at. The later new engines were thus turned out, but any good results were blanketed by the steam leakage defect so that little real improvement was achieved. It was only much later, at the very end of their lives, that a few of these engines were fitted with valve heads having six narrow rings which produced the real solution. It never occurred to anyone to apply the kind of valves which had been designed for the 2–6–0. Other attempts at improvement included trials with the 'Dabeg' feed water pump (Plate 21).

In judging the various stages in locomotive history, including this first phase of large scale amalgamation, it is necessary to exert the imagination and sense the situation in relation to the techniques available at that time. While on the one hand, viewing it from the standpoint of today's development and testing sections and research departments, the old design offices were woefully under-equipped technically, on the other hand Parkinson's Law had not then been invented and there was a long tradition of running the whole design function on a shoestring. The Lancashire and Yorkshire had, however, been one of the pioneers in building and using a Dynamometer Car, the first 4-wheeled edition having been produced in 1896. During the visit to Belgium, referred to in the last chapter, a modern car was seen with greatly increased scope in that it was able to integrate drawbar pull and speed in order to produce drawbar horsepower hours. Accordingly the L. & Y. turned out a new car of this kind from Newton Heath in 1913. Forty-two separate test runs had been carried out with it before the war started. The log book shows that these were mainly concerned with bringing up to date the resistance data worked out by Aspinall with the old car, at the turn of the century. Included in this later work was a good deal carried out with the Liverpool and Southport electric stock. After the war it was much more concerned with locomotive performance and efficiency, and it became the principal tool of comparison between the various locomotives which henceforth, and for many years to come, were run one against the other over all kinds of different routes.

In actual fact in the new Group there was a second dynamometer car, that of the old L.N.W.R., built a few years earlier. While this was also of modern bogie design it could only record speed and pull, having no integrator. Thus it produced very little of value so far as loco efficiency was concerned, and it was left unused for many years to come. There is a probably apocryphal story that Bowen Cooke used it for weekend trips to the North Wales Coast. That was about all that it was fit for at that time.

Reference has been made to the comparative tests which were carried out with L, & Y. and L.N.W. engines as the protagonists. Since Derby had no such vehicle the Horwich Car made several sallies away from home base before the Midland ‘ take-over bid ’. In July 1924, as a contribution to the discussion then going on regarding a more powerful engine for the Toton-Brent coal trains, the unique Lickey banking engine 0–10–0 No. 2290, made a run from Wellingborough to Brent. Much to my delight I was one of the crew for this test, and we met for the first time our opposite numbers from Derby with whom we were destined before long to work in daily contact. Over the performance itself it is best to draw a veil. No record appears to remain but memory recalls that it was agreed by common consent that the engine was not—repeat not—suitable for working this kind of traffic.

Other tests, the end result of which was to establish the ascendency of the Midland Compound in efficient operation are set out in Table II. Some of these have been described in the railway

Table II. Early Dynamometer car tests with Midland compounds in comparison with other types 1923-1925

Date	*Compound No.*	*Comparison with*	*Route*	*Notes*
Dec. 1923 Jan. 1924	1008	998 Mid. 2-cyl. Class 4 388 L.N.W. Prince	Leeds Carlisle	7′ 0″ Wheels*
Nov. 1924 Dec.	1065	97 Caledonian 4–4–0 124 Caledonian 4–4–0	Leeds Carlisle	6′ 9″ Wheels† Pickersgill Type
	1023	2221 L.N.W. Claughton	Leeds Carlisle	7′ 0″ Wheels*
Dec. 1924	1066			6′ 9″ Wheels†
Dec. 1924	1065	67 S. & D. 4–4–0	Bath Bournemouth	Same as Mid. Class 2
Feb. 1925	1060 1065		Leeds Carlisle	6′ 9″ Wheels† *
May 1925	1065	90 L.N.W. Prince 30 L.N.W. Claughton 10460 Horwich Rebuild	Preston Carlisle	6′ 9″ Wheels*

All tests repeated with 300 and 350 ton loads except Caledonian engines only took 300 tons, while Claughton and Horwich Rebuilt 4-cylinder 4–6–0's took 350 and 400 ton trains. The tests on the Bournemouth line were loaded to 220 tons.

* Cyls. 19″ dia. H.P. 21″ dia. L.P. × 26″

† Cyls. 19¾″ dia. H.P. 21¾″ dia. L.P. × 26″

press,[1] and the results of others have been summarised in my paper to the Institution of Locomotive Engineers in 1946. As against coal consumptions of the order of 5 lbs. per D.B.H.P. hour general with simple expansion type on the then L.M.S., the Compound ranged round 4 lbs. on comparable duties and it was little wonder that it was accepted as being head and shoulders above its contemporaries in this respect. A somewhat sour note amongst all this self congratulation was sounded by a report by Collett, published in connection with a World Power Conference about this time, to the effect that one of the new 'Castle' class locomotives on the G.W.R. had run a test train at a coal rate of 2.83 lbs. per D.B.H.P. As we could think of no earthly reason as to how this could have been achieved we simply preferred not to believe it!

This had been an intensely interesting period to an enthusiastic junior, with the opportunity it gave of learning and seeing new things tried. Academically the steady grind of three nights a week on technical studies—at the Manchester College of Technology—with one more for homework continued each winter up to and including that of 1923, when the Higher National Certificate in Mechanical Engineering was gained. This essential attainment for future progress marked the end of the more scholastic road to knowledge, and thereafter my learning took a more diverse and practical form. An early by-product was my acceptance in the year 1923 as Associate Member of the Institution of Locomotive Engineers, a body which provided an immediate window on to the wider aspects of my profession.

It is in the early twenties that it is all too easy to assume exaggerated impressions of one's own worth, with the corollary that one's superiors are failing to appreciate the treasure they possess. So it was with me, and I had various thoughts about breaking away from Horwich and going elsewhere. One such project resulted from the visit in 1923 of two brothers Dravo of Pittsburg, owning a firm of General Engineers. They came to get advice on the design of Joy's valve gear which they wished to apply to some ferry steamers on the Monongahela river, where restricted available space made this the best solution. I had something to do with them in this connection, and the next year when the senior Dravo came over to visit Wembley Exhibition he offered me passage to America and a job with the firm. After much travail of mind I finally decided not to go, primarily because it would mean leaving

[1] Reference to May 1925 Interchange Trials—O. S. Nock (*Modern Railways*, May 1963).

railway work. Although perhaps not very enterprising I did not regret this decision when four years later the great depression struck, and last in were very much first out all over the U.S.A.

In March 1925 Billington, apparently in good health, died overnight of a stroke and by the end of September, Hughes had retired. Fowler was appointed C.M.E., and by the end of the year we were made aware that the era of Midlandisation was upon us. In his first personal visit to Horwich Fowler needed a lot of persuading that it was too late to get one of the Derby standard boilers on to the 2–6–0. This happily did not take place due to the advanced state of the drawings, making of blocks and ordering of plates. He did however insist upon application of the Midland vacuum controlled steam brake and the Midland standard 3,500 gallon tender, despite the fact that it was much narrower than the cab, which had been designed to marry with quite another design of tender. He also required Derby injectors, and associated combined steam valves and clacks to be fitted. All this showed there was going to be no nonsense under the new regime about discovering the best—Midland practice was the best!

Work was stopped on the 3-cylinder 2–8–2, and we were asked to commence scheming compound versions of both this locomotive and a corresponding 4–6–2. It was also discovered that Derby had been making independent approaches as early as March 1925 to Beyer Peacock for an alternative Garratt of 2–6–0, 0–6–2 arrangement which incorporated a large number of Midland specialities.

In mid November word came to disband our little development triumvirate and Phillips was shipped off to Crewe, while Stubbs and I were commanded to start in the Derby drawing office forthwith.

Design initiative henceforth passed away from Horwich although for many years yet to come that office played its part in producing designs initiated elsewhere. It is, I think, one of the most fortunate features of my career to have been moved around to wherever design initiative was being exercised, and I was thus able to continue watching the trend of events at first hand, and sometimes even participating in them.

Because his career ended with many objectives unfulfilled, and with some Horwich products found wanting in the wider field, it may be thought that this chapter contradicts the last, where it was stated that George Hughes was a thoroughly competent engineer. It must be remembered, however, that locomotive design, with which this book principally deals, is only one segment of the whole duties of a chief mechanical engineer. Administration and maintenance of the rolling stock are by far the more important parts, and here there is another story to be told. Above all, Hughes was a product of his time, and I think of him across all these years with admiration and affection.

Table III. New steam locomotives added to L.M.S. stock during three years, 1923, 1924, 1925

	1923	*1924*	*1925*	*Totals*
Midland Designs (Eventual Standard)				
Class 4 4–4–0 3 cyl. Compound	—	40	95	135
Class 4 0–6–0 Supr. Freight	—	11	161	172
Class 3 0–6–0 Shunting Tank	—	42	8	50
	—	93	264	357
Non-Standard New Designs				
Class 5 4–6–4 Horwich Baltic Tank	—	10	—	10
Class 7 0–8–4 Crewe Freight Tank	29	1	—	30
	29	11	—	40
Existing Non-Standard Designs Perpetuated				
Class 5 4–6–0 Rebuilt Hughes 4 cyl.	21	16	4	41
Class 4 4–6–0 Prince of Wales	—	1	—	1
Class 4 4–6–0 Caledonian 14630 class	—	—	2	2
Class 3 4–4–2 'Tilbury' Tanks	10	—	5	15
Class 2 0–4–4 Caledonian Tanks	—	—	10	10
Class 7 2–8–0 Somerset and Dorset Freight	—	—	5	5
Class 3 0–6–2 North Stafford Tank	4	—	—	4
	35	17	26	78

III

The Midland Years

1926-1930

THE scene now changes, not only in the physical sense from a small railway to a large one, from Horwich on the edge of things to Derby in the centre, but also in the contact with another philosophy. Whereas Horwich and Crewe followed a relatively large engine policy, Derby had clung to the small engine. Whereas Hughes sought however imperfectly to ascertain the best, to Fowler and Anderson all that was Midland was already automatically the best. A period thus ensued in which Midland thinking and the application of Derby practices and detail were paramount, processes which have sometimes been described as 'Midlandisation'.

From 1924 to 1927 there was a three-tier stage in locomotive development, the spread of Fowler's standard Midland types overlapping what Hughes was trying to do as outlined in the last chapter, and the ideas of Anderson, the motive power chief, undermining in their turn Fowler's own proposals for new designs.

Large scale building had already begun of the Compound 4-4-0's and of the 0-6-0 Tender and Tank freight types, all of pure Midland design. During 1924 and 1925 357 of these engines had been built by Derby, Crewe and Horwich and contractors, ten times more than the number built to Hughes' designs in the same years. Consequently the newcomer's foot was already well within the door. Overnight, as it were, a block of 3,019 ex-Midland engines became 'standard' as regards their renewable parts and fittings. There was no more nonsense about 'co-ordination' and henceforth wherever existing Derby standards were applicable, there they were applied.

As in most decisions there was a good side and a bad side to all this. There is no doubt whatever that many aspects of Derby detail design were head and shoulders above that of any of the other constituents for reliable service. Special attention had been paid to good lubrication, and a general straightforward, accessible and robust design was demonstrably productive of lowest repair costs. Moreover, since boilers were well proportioned and had adequate steam space and grate areas, coal consumption was moderate in relation to the short travel valves which were universally used.

In addition, as indicated in the last chapter, the Midland held a trump card in its Compound 4–4–0 (Plate 22), of which 45 existed at the time of grouping, and 195 were built subsequently. Its simplicity and long development gave a degree of reliability and low maintenance cost in no way inferior to contemporary simple expansion engines, while its advantage in coal consumption was very real at around 20%. Although E. L. Diamond[1] has analysed the inadequacies of the short travel valve events on this engine, and has pointed out the various losses in the steam cycle which resulted, it was certainly able to work at a higher range of steam expansion than were its fellows. Also its rate of deterioration was checked since any leakage past the H.P. valves became trapped in the L.P. system and was put to useful work instead of being lost to atmosphere.

On the other hand, apart from these redoubtable machines, some of the other types were distinctly feeble. There were one or two skeletons in the cupboard, such as the Deely 0–6–4 Tank which had to retire so ignominiously from the fray when the Midland took over the Tilbury section. The whole relative situation was rather well summed up by a Midland man when he wrote of this period.[2]

"At Derby the nice little engines were made pets of. They were housed in nice clean sheds and were very lightly loaded. There must have been a Royal Society for the Prevention of Cruelty to Engines in existence. At Horwich they had gone all scientific and talked in 'thous' although apparently some of their work was to the nearest half inch. At Crewe they just didn't care so long as their engines could roar and rattle along with a good paying load, which they usually did."

Sir Henry Fowler had been knighted for his contribution to the war effort in other than railway matters, and his prime interests were in administration, workshops and metallurgy. To put no fine point upon it Fowler was not very interested in locomotive design, as apart from locomotive policy, and I hardly ever remember seeing him in the Drawing Office. I never as a matter of fact had any words with him at all during my whole stay at Derby, and

[1] "Investigations into the Cylinder Losses in a Compound Locomotive"—E. L. Diamond (*Proceedings* Inst. Mech. Engrs. 1927).

[2] D. W. Sanford's contribution to paper "A Modern Locomotive History" (*Proceedings* Inst. Loco. Engrs. No. 190, 1946).

although this was normal enough perhaps in the bigger organisation, it was a change from Horwich where Hughes contrived to meet and speak to even quite junior people.

I do not, of course, for this reason discount Sir Henry as an engineer, and there are those who were trained or served under him who hold his memory in high regard. I do, however, from personal knowledge confirm what Hamilton Ellis says in his book on the Midland Railway[1] that it is doubtful whether Fowler ever designed a locomotive. The only relevant writing under his name is concerned with components.[2]

In charge of all design work was Herbert Chambers, a really attractive personality, who presided over a drawing office situated just under the Clock Tower in what are now the Derby Locomotive Works offices. This was divided into two sections, the older and main section under 'Jock' Henderson, and the other under 'Jock' Campbell. The two 'Jocks' of unmistakable nationality, but quite opposite temperaments and appearances, were the residue of importations fron the far north made when Anderson had been Chief Draughtsman in earlier days. Since they held between them the key positions under the chief there was a good deal of thwarted ambition amongst the resident Sassenachs!

Unlike Crewe or Horwich, Derby Drawing Office had a clear cut and separate experimental section, which accounted for its much more purposeful lead in principles and practices. D. W. Sanford was in charge, a bluff and hearty Wiltshireman, as much respected for his sense of humour as for his B.A. (Cantab.)—a very rare attainment in railway drawing offices of that day. Under him dealing, more particularly with tests of the actual locomotives on the footplate, was 'Uncle' Sutherland, one of the many unsung backroom heroes of the art. He was only surpassed by Jimmy Doleman of the general part of the office, who had his clothes cut in Edwardian fashion, and who carried an old-world courtesy which stood out like a beacon light amongst the rough and tumble of office life. Also in the experimental section was Edgar Larkin, eventually to become first Director of Work Study to the then far distant British Transport Commission, and still later Deputy General Manager, Workshops. An evening visitor to the office when we were on overtime was Roland Bond, one day to be C.M.E. of the whole of British Railways and President of the Institute of Mechanical

[1] *The Midland Railway*—C. Hamilton Ellis (Ian Allan 1953).
[2] "Superheated Steam in Locomotives"—H. Fowler (*Proc.* Inst. Civil Engrs. Vol. CXCVI 1913/14).

Engineers, who at that time was working on a boiler design as part of his thesis for membership of the 'Civils'.

The atmosphere and the personalities at Derby were extraordinarily congenial to me, which helped a lot to counterbalance the fall in my fortunes. At Horwich I had built up something of a special position for myself whereas here, for the first year at any rate, I reverted to an ordinary pencil pusher in the body of the office. However by early 1927 I had connected again with Dynamometer Car work. From October in that year I was put in charge of all of this testing work in the field—acting under Sanford of the experimental section to which I was then transferred. Here I remained until the termination of my first spell at Derby at the end of 1930.

Formality and horse-play lived side by side in the old office. At the end of my career, although in executive rank I address those of still senior position as 'Freddie', 'Roland' or 'John'. But in 1926 in the Derby Drawing Office all in authority were 'Sir' and colleagues were invariably 'Mister' all the way from leading draughtsman Armin, a man of quiet competent dignity, to poor old Briggs, the office butt, whose waking thoughts dwelt in York Minster whence he repaired every week-end to act as unpaid guide. Memory recalls the devilish office boy who would laboriously excavate a knot hole in an absent draughtsman's desk top, patiently fish with a piece of wire for his drawing instruments, carefully file all the points blunt, and then restore everything to seeming innocence. One remembers the endless wrangles about windows open and windows shut, and the incursions of the girl clerks—a welcome diversion to the young men and a solace to the old—the conduct of both parties being held within bounds by the infinite possibilities of ridicule. I recall the glorious chaos when, some time in 1928, the whole office contents were removed to new accommodation on the ground floor of an adjacent building and a group commenting in Rabelaisian terms upon the apparition of Sir Henry himself, clad in Scout leader's uniform on the occasion of the christening of one of the 'Royal Scot' engines as 'The Boy Scout'. These and a hundred other memories are the stuff of which the lighter side of Drawing Office life consists.

Although the operating side were so satisfied with existing Midland types for any foreseeable traffic, there had clearly been rumblings in Sir Henry's mind towards a new larger engine. In 1924 a diagram had been prepared for an enlarged Midland 3-cylinder 4–6–0 Compound shown in Fig. 6. This is one of the few of

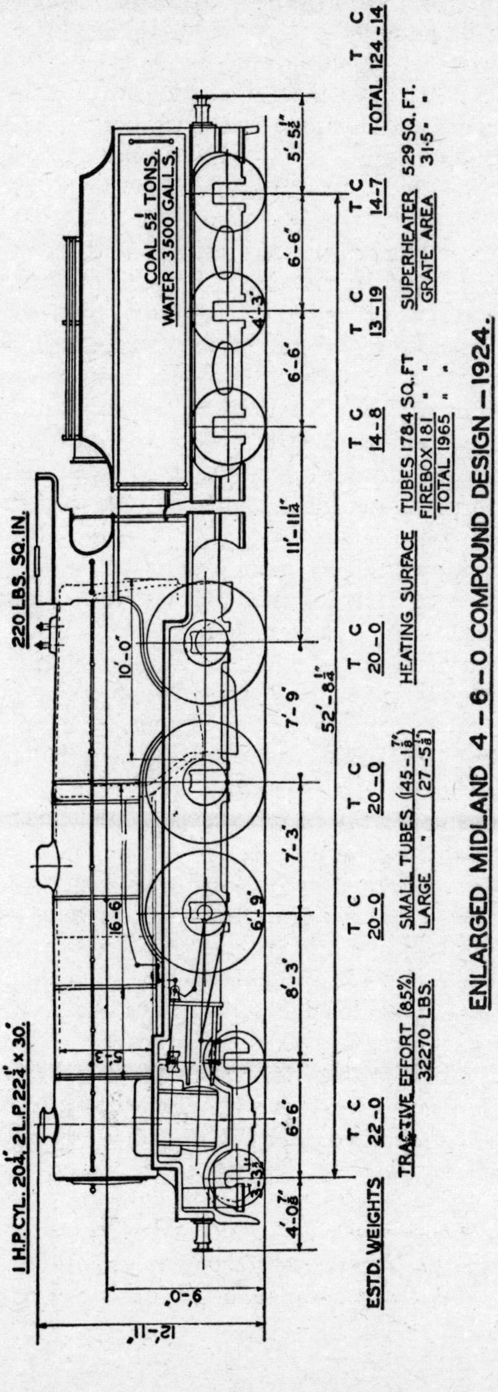
1 H.P. CYL. 20¼" 2 L.P. 22¼" x 30"
220 LBS. SQ. IN.
COAL 5¾ TONS
WATER 3500 GALLS.
12'-11"
9'-0"
16'-6
10'-0"
5'-3
6'-9"
4'-3"
4'-0⅞"
6'-6"
8'-3"
7'-3"
7'-9"
11'-11¼"
6'-6"
6'-6"
5'-5⅞"
52'-8¼"
ESTD. WEIGHTS
T C 22-0
T C 20-0
T C 20-0
T C 20-0
T C 14-8
T C 13-19
T C 14-7
T C TOTAL 124-14
TRACTIVE EFFORT (85%) 32270 LBS.
SMALL TUBES (145-1⅞") LARGE " (27-5⅛")
HEATING SURFACE TUBES 1784 SQ. FT FIREBOX 181 " " TOTAL 1965 " "
SUPERHEATER 529 SQ. FT. GRATE AREA 31·5 " "
ENLARGED MIDLAND 4-6-0 COMPOUND DESIGN—1924.

Fig. 6

those early projects which one can really regret was not followed up. Not only would they have been handsome engines, but there seems no reason why they could not have equalled the performance of the eventual 'Royal Scot', even if at a lower level of efficiency. A generous grate area and adequate firebox volume were supported by ample ashpan capacity and proper provision for combustion air entry, thus avoiding the weak link in so many of the other large 4–6–0's about the country.

Some old correspondence remains dealing with the means by which this idea for a large compound became grafted upon the Hughes 4–6–2 schemes and led to the ghostly compound Pacific, which very nearly came to be built somewhere about the end of 1926. It appears that immediately upon Hughes' retirement a deputation was sent out to visit France in October 1925. This consisted of Sir Henry himself, with Gass of Horwich, and Bulleid, then of the L.N.E.R. no doubt acting as interpreter. They visited all of the French main line railways, but did not, to their surprise, find a 100% acceptance of the Compound principle, Bachellery of the Midi, Lacoin of the P.O. and Nasse of the Etat dissenting. However Vallentin of the P.L.M., Buchatel, Est, and Collin, Nord, plus Dubois of the Central Design Office spoke in favour with strong if somewhat diverse voices. They claimed a general 10 to 15% fuel advantage over simple expansion in everyday working, at an extra cost in repairs of only some 8% of the value of the coal saved. Their advice differed as to boiler pressure, ratio of cylinder volumes, independent or combined valve gears and receiver capacity.

The evidence was thought sufficiently encouraging to go ahead, and a design team was organised forthwith to progress the matter. Gass took the lead at Horwich with cylinders and valve gear, Chambers tackled the boiler at Derby and Grover, Chief Draughtsman at Crewe, came in on the detail work. A meeting at Derby on October 23rd, 1925, settled the main details, which were set out in one of the last schemes I worked upon before leaving Horwich and illustrated by Fig. 7. Apart from what is indicated on this diagram, 9″ dia. piston valves were proposed for H.P. and 11″ for L.P. The drive was divided and two sets of outside Walschaert gear operated the four valves. Separate H.P. and L.P. gears were ruled out because it was felt that both by training and temperament it was unlikely that British drivers would make full use of independent cut offs. A starting valve was proposed, based upon that used on the old L. & Y. 0–8–0 compounds, consisting of a small slide

Plate 16. Highland Railway 'Snaigow' class 4–4–0 No. 74 *Durn* leaves Inverness with the afternoon express for Wick.

Plate 17. Midland Railway Johnson unrebuilt 4–4–0 No. 322 piloting a Class 3 0–6–0 on a southbound coal train near Ribblehead. Notice the fireman of No. 322 attending to the valve gear while the train is moving.

Plate 18. Horwich 2–6–0 No. 42855 heads a down express freight train at Elstree, 33 years after building.

Plate 19. Dynamometer Car trials with a typical Toton-Brent coal train in 1928, double-headed by Class 3 and Class 4 0–6–0 locomotives.

Plate 20. No. 10467, one of the last series of Hughes' four-cylinder superheated 4–6–0s, leaves Carlisle with an up West Coast express.

Plate 21. Test of Hughes' four-cylinder superheated 4–6–0 with 'Dabeg' feed water pump (1927). Left to right: M. A. Henstock (Derby); G. (later Sir George) Briggs (Dabeg Co.); R. I. Kirkland (Horwich); J. C. Loach (Horwich); T. F. B. Simpson (Horwich).

Plate 22. Preparing for the test. Midland compound No. 1094 and the Horwich Dynamometer Car at Nottingham shed.

Plate 23. Hughes' four cylinder 4–6–0 No. 10456 converted to compound operation.

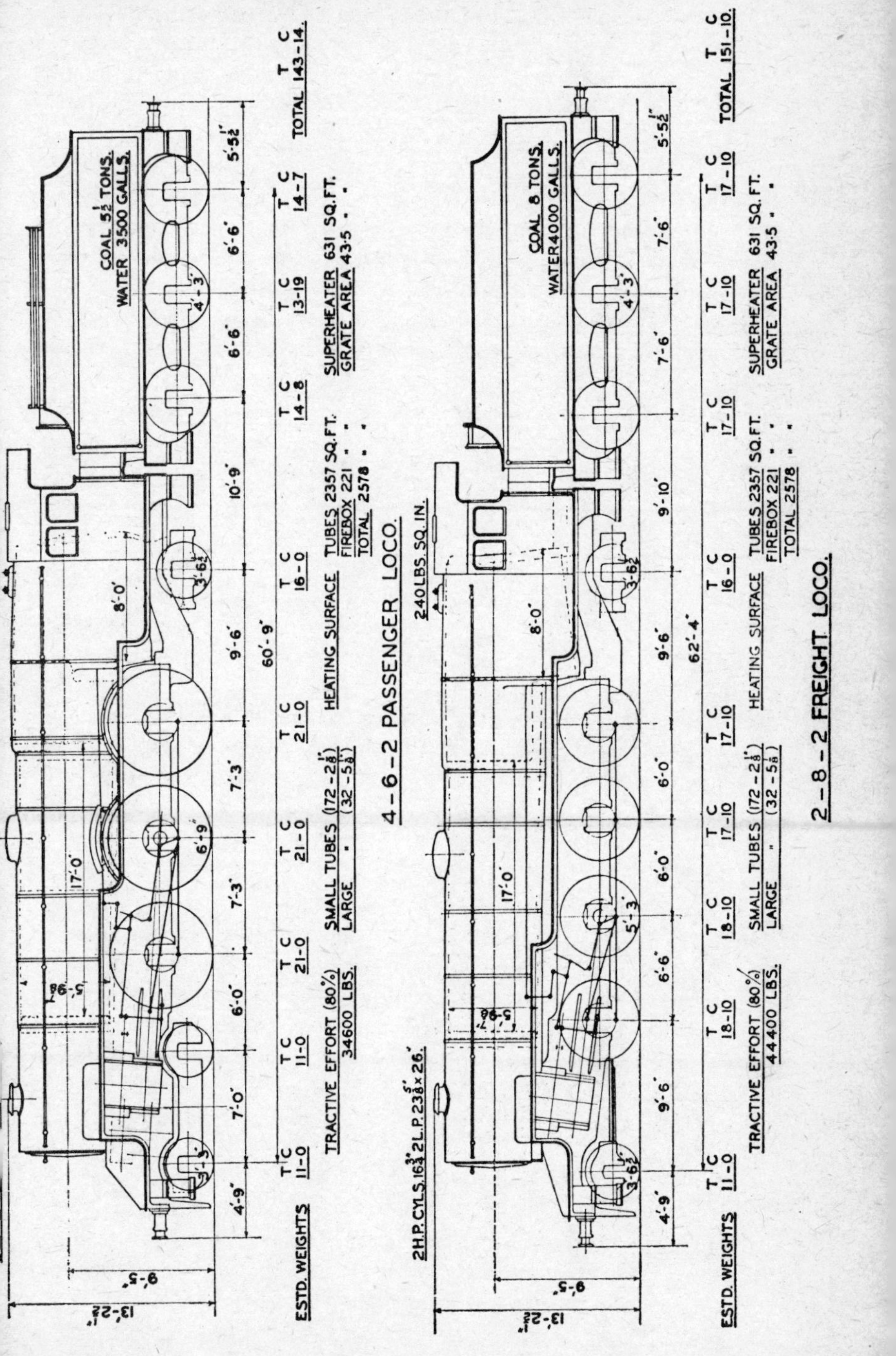

4-6-2 PASSENGER LOCO.

2-8-2 FREIGHT LOCO.

valve within the L.P. cylinder casting. This was coupled to the reversing shaft in such a manner that when cut off was within 5% of full gear, forwards or backwards, a port was uncovered admitting H.P. steam to the L.P. cylinders. One other feature of interest lay in the firebox. In order to keep tube length to the reasonable figure of 17′ a combustion chamber of no less than 4′ in length was provided. However, as this involved a circumferential riveted seam right round the copper inner firebox, and a very small radius was provided at the throat, it is possible that the whole arrangement could have proved troublesome in maintenance.

The corresponding 2–8–2 for the Toton to Brent service (Fig. 8) was developed simultaneously using the same boiler and details, but here the cylinders all drove on to the same axle.

While this work was proceeding in the three offices it was also decided to convert one of the Hughes 4–6–0's to compound expansion following the same general principles, and No. 10456 (Plate 23) was turned out of Horwich in July 1926, with new inside cylinders of 22″ dia. 9″ dia. piston valves were retained and the existing outside cylinders were lineared up to 15½″ dia. Boiler pressure remained at 180 lbs. Although the latter value was a handicap compared with the 240 lbs. per sq. in. intended for the large engines, the work of this 'guinea pig' is of interest as indicating how the 'Pacific' might have behaved.

No. 10456 spent its life on the Crewe-Carlisle line, was very free running, and was well liked by the drivers. On test with 350 ton trains it showed 26% coal saving over similar locomotives as built with the original leaky piston valves, but only 9% over the same engine as ultimately fitted with valve heads having six narrow rings. On the other hand its best efficiency was nearly 20% below that ultimately attained by the Royal Scot.

The big engines might have done better than this because of their higher pressure, but on the whole I have always felt it fortunate that they were never built. Pre-Chapelon as they were, they could not exploit compound expansion to the full, while undersized axle bearings, solid crankshafts, and the boiler details mentioned above were all features which could have affected their reliability and maintenance cost. A foundation ring and some flanging blocks were made and, although I never actually saw them, there seems little doubt that some cylinders were cast. Design work was well advanced with a lot of material ordered before the dramatic order came to stop everything. No trace now remains of all this activity excepting the four-ply frame construction at the back end over the trailing truck which principle was incorporated into the eventual Stanier Pacifics.

There is a rather widely held belief that C.M.E.'s of old were veritable giants of power who dictated to General Managers and operating departments alike. This idea probably stemmed from the careers of such awe-inspiring characters as Webb and Drummond, while in later times Gresley established seemingly effortless ascendency in a much more urbane manner. I cannot truthfully say that such was the case however with any of the C.M.E.'s under whom I have worked. Consider in this connection what now befell Sir Henry Fowler—the two largest prestige locomotive designs which he had sponsored to the hilt, and on which work was proceeding at full bore in three drawing offices was halted, and alternatives were proposed by others, accepted by Management, and brought to fulfilment, which owed nothing to the initiative of Fowler himself or his people. What a fascinating story it might have made to identify the first doubts, to follow the conversations and correspondence, and to chart step by step this amazing *volte face*. All that remains are a few dry, factual, Board minutes—the protagonists have all departed, and the written and verbal warfare, which it is to be assumed had taken place, has long since vanished, unless some unknown antiquary, rooting amidst the rubble of old Euston, has saved something from the ruins with which to startle posterity.

The facts appear to have been as follows. As already indicated Anderson in charge of motive power was a man of strong character. By the early part of 1926 he was forced to acknowledge, in company with his overlord, J. H. Follows, that 4–4–0 Midland Compounds simply would not suffice for the Anglo Scottish service. Because the Compound had been by far the most successful design on the Midland he had a strong belief in the superiority of 3 cylinders as such and a shadow of this view had, as already described, fallen upon the original Hughes 4-cylinder Pacific scheme to turn it into a 3-cylinder scheme before its final demise. Anderson also believed in the least number of wheels to do the job and, more practically perhaps, was dismayed by the number of new 65′ or 70′ turntables which would be needed were a Pacific to be adopted. There was already in the country a 4–6–0, albeit of 4 rather than 3 cylinder arrangement, whose excellent performance and efficiency in comparison with its contemporaries was there for all to see, namely the G.W.R. 'Castle' class. Anderson and Follows evidently persuaded the Management to apply for loan of one of these engines so that in September 1926, while the design of Fowler's Pacific was still in full flight, No. 5000 'Launceston Castle' was brought over to the L.M.S. First of all used between Euston and Crewe, it subsequently ran on the Carlisle road and on this latter route was the subject of Dynamometer car trials at which I was fortunate enough to be present. Throughout the whole exercise No. 5000 performed with quiet mastery all the work on which the Claughtons, often piloted, lost time, dropped their steam pressure, and made the welkin ring with their reverberating exhaust. It displayed the full measure of the extent to which Bowen Cooke had failed to absorb the lesson of the earlier G.W.-L.N.W. locomotive exchange in 1910, which was the forerunner of the Claughton design.

Train loads of 400 and 430 tons were taken on successive round trips, the engine usually gaining from 7 to 11 mins. on a schedule of 164 mins. for the 141 miles. On one occasion however 6 mins. were lost between Oxenholme and Tebay due to persistent slipping in bad weather, a rather unusual failing for this class. Pressure was held almost faultlessly throughout the series, a cutoff of 22% being maintained on the more level sections, with part open regulator. Cutoff was generally opened out to 27% at Grayrigg and 35% at Shap Summit going north and to 30% at the latter point coming south. Coal consumption averaged 3.8 lbs. per D.B.H.P. hour, which was better than anything yet seen on the L.M.S., even on the Midland Compounds, and notwithstanding the low degree superheat then common in all G.W.R. practice. The Dynamometer Car report concluded with the words "As regards efficiency it will be noted that whereas the rates of combustion and evaporation were in no way exceptional, the coal and steam consumptions were very good and this would indicate that the efficiency of the Great Western engine results from the engine portion and economical accessory fittings, and as a result of this the boiler is well able to produce the steam required at low fuel consumption".

It then listed seven individual features which led to this good result. Plate 24 shows 'Launceston Castle' outside the old Midland Durran Hill shed at Carlisle taken during the course of these trials.

Although none of us at Derby heard of it, apparently it next became the wish of the L.M. Board to have built 50 locomotives to the G.W.R. design, but there were difficulties in the way, including that of loading gauge. A 3-cylinder 4–6–0 having a maximum size boiler, high steam pressure, high degree superheat and long travel valve gear was quickly decided upon in lieu. Partly because the Derby drawing office was by then embarked upon another design as will shortly be described, partly because the new locomotives were wanted for the very next summer, the order was placed at the end of 1926 upon the North British Locomotive Company. The resources of their large design office and of their Hyde Park and Queens Park works were concentrated upon the new project with the result that the first engine was turned out in August 1927, and the whole order for the first 50 were on the road by the end of that year. Thus was born the well known 'Royal Scot' class (Plate 25).

At the time of my transfer to Derby and until August 1926 work was very slack in the Drawing Office. The design of the 'Pacific' boiler, above mentioned, only occupied one section, and the rest, including myself, had to exist on a diet of scraps. Not only this, but to eke out the time and to keep the staff together against future demands, the section leaders were instructed to impose a 'go slow' procedure which consisted of requiring the men to re-scheme even the simplest jobs over and over again, until the utmost ingenuity could conceive of no further alternatives. This was a desperately thwarting procedure to the youngsters who for the most part were raring to go places, but it was an accepted feature of office life to the older men who had encountered it often before. During this spell I did a bit on alternative tubeplate and firebox arrangements for the Claughtons, which had to be kept going until the new engines could take their place. Derby had some idea of sending along an improved boiler scheme which would revolutionise the indifferent steaming. As they did not yet realise that the trouble lay in the valvery—eventually to be transformed by the application of solid valve heads with six narrow rings—and also in the low position of the firebox foundation ring which stifled air supply, it is not surprising that they did not have much success at this stage. A useful effort was the redesign of the standard Horwich version of the 'Ross' pop safety valve, to come within 8½" total height. This was done specifically for the Pacifics, but was applied to the 'Scots' and became the L.M. standard for all large engines. Another of my jobs was to design lower extension arms for the regulator handles of Compounds and Class 4 Freight engines. As these types spread onto other divisions the men revolted at their having to grope almost on tiptoe up in the cab-roof to find the handles, and they demanded means of operation which were more natural to the human stance, and which even, tell it not in Gath, could be worked sitting down.

An interlude in all this was provided by the General Strike. Union membership had been a 'must' at Horwich, and I had joined first of all the forerunner of the A.E.U. while I was in the workshops, and then the Technical section of the Railway Clerks Association when I entered the drawing office. Although the early twenties are usually the 'leftest' portion of many people's lives, I am afraid that deep political conscience does not always settle upon the minds of young men so soon. It arose therefore that compared with the prospect of getting out on the footplate of the engines providing the attenuated strike services, the rights and wrongs of the social problem occupied a reprehensibly low place in my mind. With Sanford as driver I thus spent happy days firing on Nos. 495, 174 and 527 preparing, coaling, and watering our own engines, and making forays in the Leicester and Rowsley directions, and shunting Derby station yard (Plate 26). After such defiant action in the face of strike orders, my days of union membership came to an end.

In August the under-employed part of the office was turned on to the design of a 2–6–4 Tank engine, which as the Pacific project lapsed, came to occupy the whole of the men. The need for a good general-purpose tank engine, already voiced in 1922, and unsatisfied by the Horwich 'Baltic' Tank, had become more insistent, and its layout formed itself almost automatically. The first act in designing any six-coupled engine at Derby at that time was to lay down wheel centres spaced at 8′ 0″ and 8′ 6″, dimensions which had become sacred with the passage of time. In this instance the next move was to choose an existing standard boiler, namely the G8AS otherwise used on the Class 3, 4–4–0's. The key decision, which assured that this engine would become a really successful type was to design brand new cylinders with straight ports, adequate size of piston valves, and long-lap Walschaert valve gear. I think the already designed Horwich 2–6–0 had some influence here, although the motion details were based upon that of the Derby designed Somerset & Dorset 2–8–0's. The tanks, cab and bunker, the design of which was entrusted to me as a group, were to be based upon those of the ill-starred 0–6–4 Derby tanks. Thus was assembled a design which became instantly successful when turned out in 1927, and which in due course spread far and wide over L.M. metals.

While the above activity was on, the design of the Royal Scot began in Glasgow, and Chambers and some of his senior henchmen made regular trips north, bearing drawings of Derby practice of all kinds for inclusion in the new engine. The author has in the past indulged in some little controversy with H. Holcroft, late of the G.W. and Southern Railways, as to wherein lay the inspiration and roots of this design, the former claiming a large measure of G.W. ancestry while the latter has stated that it owed more to the Southern 'Lord Nelson', by that time already in traffic. As in most such arguments there is a measure of truth on both sides, and the facts seem to have been as follows. The trials of the G.W. Castle over the L.M. fixed the decision for a non-compound 4–6–0. Anderson's predilections settled the 3-cylinders. It is true that a set of drawings of the 'Lord Nelson' were sought and obtained for transmission to Glasgow. Of these the firebox was used almost intact, although this in turn had been inspired by the G.W. influence brought to Ashford by Holcroft himself, among others. Apart from this the 'Nelson' style of cab was followed, but the closest inspection of relative design feature does not disclose any other way in which the 'Nelson' influenced the 'Scot'. The cylinders and valve gear were directly derived from those of the 2–6–4 Tank, whilst the rest of the layout incorporated Midland standard details in profusion, including bogie brakes and cylinder bye-pass valves. Although the coupled axleboxes were of manganese bronze with brass and white metal inserts, this being normal Midland practice, they were fortunately given really generous dimensions and were mechanically lubricated. The only discernible feature from the ex-L.N.W. main line over which they were destined to work was the crosshead driven vacuum pump. Twenty more of these engines were built at Derby in 1930.

Thus after travail stretching over 4 years a large modern express passenger engine at last became available on the L.M.S. main lines and the good use to which it was put has been amply chronicled elsewhere. Although much of a hybrid in its new, then modified and finally rebuilt form this engine must be counted as one of the major successes of the steam era, and it would be interesting to know the net earnings of these 70 machines during their whole lives.

What, then, of the corresponding heavy freight engine for the Toton to Brent Coal traffic which has appeared like a theme song throughout this story since the amalgamation? Here again the dichotomy inherent in the set-up of the L.M. mechanical department manifested itself, and it was discovered that Anderson, and not Fowler, had initialed the contracts with Beyer Peacocks. From information kindly supplied through Maurice Crane of that firm, it can be established that the Derby proposals were initiated in March 1925, simultaneously with those from Horwich, and Gorton for a time was in the unique position of developing separate schemes for two different parts of the same railway! Moreover it was the Motive Power Superintendent and not the Deputy C.M.E. who held technical meetings and visited the firm. It was only in September that Fowler was at last brought into the picture after his accession as C.M.E. of the whole group, but he was clearly only a 'front' to Anderson who continued to direct operations from the rear.

The development work done at Horwich on long-lap valve gears was completely ignored, and there is a record that the same cylinder and valve gear arrangement as was used on the Somerset and Dorset 2–8–0, having only $3\frac{3}{4}''$ travel, was insisted upon, Anderson himself having developed this when he was in charge of design. Worst of all the generous sized bearings, already in use on the Horwich 2–6–0 and selected by the Derby office itself for the Royal Scot and 2–6–4 Tank currently under design, were jettisoned for no other reason than an almost mindless addiction to all things Midland. Beyer Peacocks made a particular feature of good bearing sizes in all of their own Garratt designs, and they plead vigorously for some latitude. But no, as a maximum concession they were permitted to use boxes 8″ dia. × 9″ long on the coupled wheels instead of the $8\frac{1}{2}''$ dia. × $8\frac{1}{4}''$ long boxes which were asked for. The driving boxes on the Horwich engines were $8\frac{1}{2}''$ dia. × $10\frac{7}{8}''$ long. Three of these engines were delivered in 1927, and with 45,620 lbs. tractive effort they hauled single handed the coal trains, for so long double headed, at the same average overall speed of 17 m.p.h. between the Derbyshire pits and the metropolis. Rather naturally they gave no specific coal saving over the earlier 0–6–0's and their inadequate axleboxes wore rapidly and brought the engines into the shops for repairs at less than half the mileage which would have been possible had already available design features been adopted.

They were all in all a poor advertisement for the Garratt principle to which further reference is made in Chapter IV.

It was in this era that the battle of the valves was fought and eventually won on the L.M.S. These superficially minor changes from short lap to long lap, from single or at most double stiff wide rings to more numerous flexible narrow rings, were in fact amongst the really profound influences which changed steam locomotive performance and efficiency out of all recognition. The first of them promoted more expansive use of steam, with enhanced freedom of exhaust, while the latter ensured minimum internal steam leakage from steam to exhaust areas, and sustained this property without marked deterioration for periods of 30 to 40,000 miles between examinations. In terms of economy, the long-lap valves produced a general saving of 25% in coal per drawbar horsepower hour, a good deal more than was claimed by the French engineers for compounding. A dramatic example of the effect of internal leakage was the case of the 'Royal Scots' which, when first put to work, did the 300 miles through run from Euston to Carlisle on 5 tons of coal. Two years later, notwithstanding their good valve events, they were using 9 tons. However high the tenders were stacked it was a struggle to win through. The engine men experienced many anxious moments, and the running of the trains was affected in consequence.

This woeful experience accelerated the work on which Sanford and his men had been engaged for some time, the outcome of which was that No. 6158 was eventually fitted with valve heads each having six plain narrow rings ¼″ in width, and tests proved that 30,000 miles could be run before examination with a deterioration of only 8% instead of the 80% previously experienced (Fig. 9E).

Not only was this arrangement adopted as standard for future construction, but it was eventually applied retrospectively to almost all of the 'standard' types having a high life expectation. It was also applied to some of the last of the Claughtons and Hughes' rebuilt 4–6–0's, so that in their final days, as they were being taken off the more important services, they both displayed the efficiency of which they were intrinsically capable—but too late to re-establish their true worth. It was rather sad!

These improvements appear both simple and self-evident today, but the resistance offered to the adoption of long-lap valves from various sources was extraordinarily tenacious. Against all evidence it was claimed that wear of valves and motion pins would be excessive, ignoring the fact that the actual movement of long travel valves at short cut-off was almost identical with that of short travel valves at long cut-off which was the habitual mode of working with the latter. The facts that the G.W. had used long lap since the turn of the century, that Clayton, high priest of Midland design until he went to Ashford in 1914 had adopted it in 1917, and that its effects were there for all to see in no less than three new L.M.S. designs did nothing to deflect the minds of the opposition which centred in the person of 'Jock' Campbell in charge of section two of the Drawing Office. Neither Fowler nor Chambers saw matters clearly enough to exert their authority with the unseemly result that, apart from the Garratts, the next two new designs undertaken at Derby had short travel valve gear, namely the Class 2 4–4–0 and Class 3 2–6–2 Tank.

The strange part of it all was that there was no disagreement that valve events required improving—it was simply that to do this by increasing the travel was deemed intolerable. For many years all Crewe-built engines had been fitted with an auxiliary port in each piston valve head (known for some strange reason as a 'trick' port), the effect of which was intended to double steam admission for a given nominal opening. Inspection of Fig. 9A shows that this idea could only be partly effective due to wiredrawing, but it did undoubtedly act as a kind of supercharger and contribute to some of the heroic and historic L.N.W.R. performances. The trouble was that the increased steam input had no increase in opportunity to get out of the cylinders again and the resultant high back pressure was one cause of the supreme noisiness of Crewe engines.

Beames, the C.M.E. *manqué* at Crewe, sat surlily in that citadel of past glories and viewed with a sour gaze all that went on at Derby, and with a still more jaundiced eye any instructions appertaining to locomotive design which arrived from that despised headquarters. Very naturally he would have liked to have been designing his own engines, and that he had some novel ideas on the subject soon began to emerge. A memo of the 10th November, 1925, records that he commented upon Fowler's proposed Pacific saying that it ought to have 6′ 3″ dia. instead of 6′ 9″ wheels, also that it ought to be arranged so that it could be worked either simple or compound at the driver's discretion, and that it should have no splashers, but a simple running board running from cab front to smokebox front. This latter theme he subsequently developed in a proposal to debag the Claughtons, and I certainly saw a drawing to this effect, showing a single thin running board high up above the coupled wheels. Unfortunately all further trace of this early step towards 'austerity' in locomotive appearance seems to have been lost.

Beames's satisfactory studies of the Caprotti poppet valve gear recently introduced into Italy are more significant. Theoretically it was ideal in the ready manner in which it permitted any desired valve events to be obtained, and it attained by alternative means

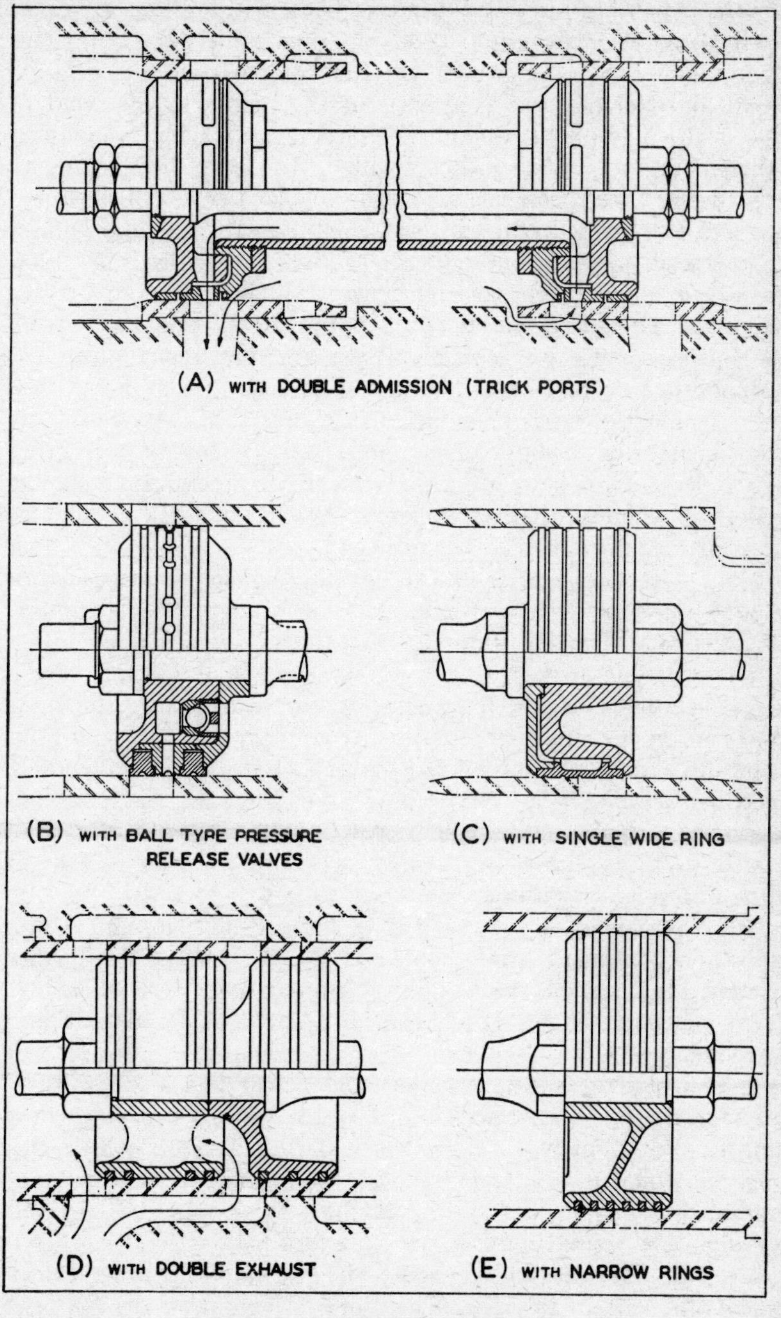

TYPES OF PISTON VALVE HEADS L.78

Fig. 9

the same virtues which had been reached with piston valves as described above. Claughton 5908 was thus equipped resulting in a triumphant 20% coal saving on test compared to the original design, and Beames was converted to the merits of this kind of valve gear and upheld it staunchly for the rest of his time. Ten further Claughtons were so dealt with in this way, in addition to the fitting of larger boilers having 200 in place of 175 lbs. per sq. in. pressure. These produced a 27% fuel saving over the originals, but it was all too late since the alternatives of narrow ring piston valves and long travel valve gear were capable of even greater savings, at a reduced initial cost. Although further essays were made with poppet valve gears about this time they never succeeded in demonstrating any commanding superiority.

Now came the last dying kick of the anti-long-travel brigade. It was primarily invented by Sanford, as a means of conferring upon older engines, already built with short travel gear, a similar freedom of exhaust to that conferred by the long travel, and as shown in Fig. 9D consisted of an inversion of the old L.N.W. trick port, to give double area of exit for the exhaust steam through the liners. As in the former case much of this supposed advantage was lost in wiredrawing through the tortuous passages, and in fact nothing like the expected efficiency was ever obtained. These valves eventually became highly unpopular with the shed staffs, for when carbon had built up on the circumference of the heads and behind the rings, the added surface of contact often made them exceedingly difficult to extract from the liners for examination. Nevertheless these double exhaust valves as they were called were applied to three classes of new construction, over the details of which Campbell was able to maintain control.

Fowler remained in command until the end of 1930, and design inspiration continued firmly rooted in Derby. All of the further locomotives designed and built in this period were therefore, except for the Class 7 0–8–0's, truly in the old Midland tradition. No sooner was the 2–6–4 Tank design previously mentioned well on the way, than a smaller general purpose tank was proposed and at first eyes were turned upon the admirable 0–6–2 and 0–6–4 Tank engines, already in service on the North Stafford constituent. It simply would not do to perpetuate one of these since it was non-standard in every detail. So a Midland version was planned, and its design was carried quite a long way forward on the lines shown in Fig. 10. The centrepiece had to be one of the existing Derby standard boilers, in this case a superheated version of the G6 used

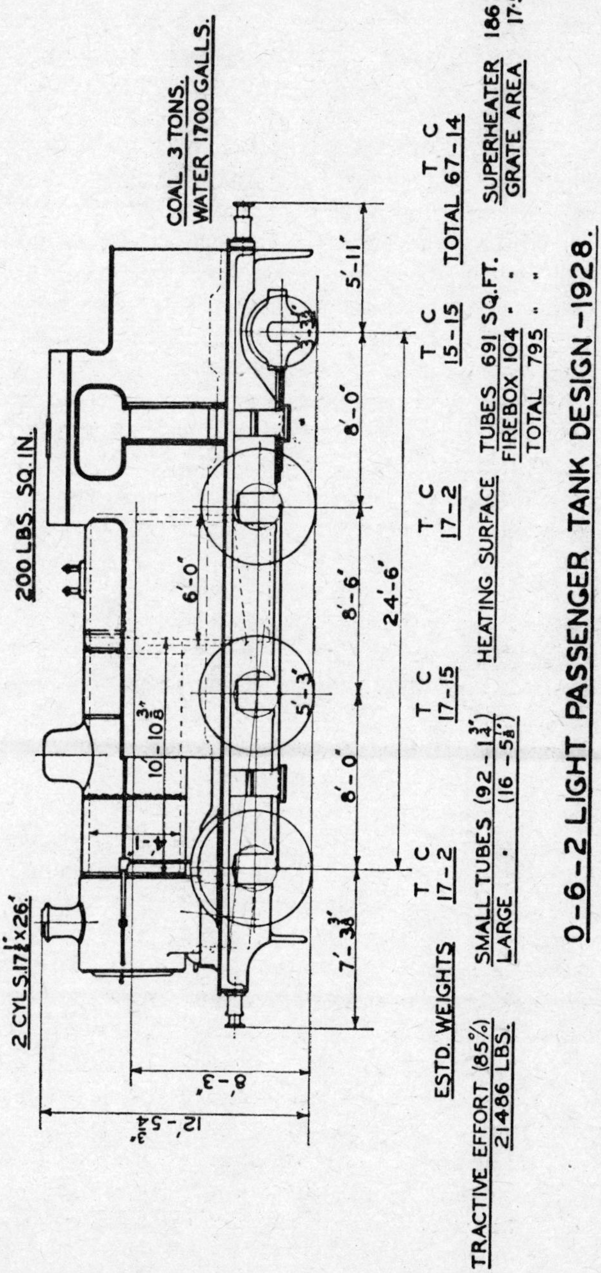

200 LBS. SQ. IN.
COAL 3 TONS.
WATER 1700 GALLS.
2 CYLS. 17½" x 26"
12'-5¾"
8'-3"
10'-10⅜"
4'-1"
6'-0"
5'-3"
7'-3⅜"
8'-0"
8'-6"
8'-0"
5'-11"
24'-6"
ESTD. WEIGHTS
T C 17-2
T C 17-15
T C 17-2
T C 15-15
T C TOTAL 67-14
TRACTIVE EFFORT (85%) 21486 LBS.
SMALL TUBES (92 - 1¾")
LARGE " (16 - 5⅛")
HEATING SURFACE
TUBES 691 SQ.FT.
FIREBOX 104 " "
TOTAL 795 " "
SUPERHEATER 186 SQ.FT.
GRATE AREA 17·5 " "
0-6-2 LIGHT PASSENGER TANK DESIGN-1928.

Fig. 10

on the smaller Midland 0–6–0's. Inside Walschaerts gear was to be a novel departure but needless to say providing only short travel. However, the resultant $17\frac{3}{4}$ ton maximum axle load was considered too severe for bridge loading in connection with the desired route availability and a fresh start had to be made with a 2–6–2 version, which would give a better distribution of the total weight.

A 2–6–2 tank had been a Derby dream over many years right back to Deeley's time and there were in the archives diagrams of at least half a dozen previous attempts which had come to nothing—some of them of the most fearsome aspect. Now, and finally, in 1930 one of the feeblest locomotives of modern times was produced, under boilered, carrying too much deadweight for its power, and retaining a thoroughly inefficient front end, for which use of the double exhaust valves did practically nothing to remedy (Plate 27). It was designed in a portion of the same office, divided only by a partition from the other part, which had already produced the entirely excellent 2–6–4 Tank. I think this fact is some evidence that Fowler, who after all was finally responsible, did not have any very clear ideas on locomotive design as such, whatever his other abilities.

Even the most rabid Derby-ite could not but acknowledge that the Midland Class 2 engine was not very bright. For loads under 200 tons, or double headed under 350 tons it at least ran the railway but there was no sting about its performance. Indicator diagrams in the shape of very thin bananas showed severe throttling at both inlet and exhaust, and were the sign of a thoroughly constipated front end. The valves, undersized in relation to the cylinder diameter of $20\frac{1}{2}''$ were placed underneath and were driven directly by short travel Stephenson's gear. There were three ways in which improvement could be made for future new construction. First, the cylinders could be brought outside, and a scheme was actually worked out to do this. Loading gauge difficulties on secondary lines were too restrictive, and a second alternative was resorted to, leaving the general arrangement the same, but redesigning the cylinder block to improve the ports and passages. This was done in Campbell's part of the Drawing Office leaving the underneath position of the valves unaltered, but the 19″ instead of $20\frac{1}{2}''$ dia. cylinders possible due to lifting the pressure to 180 lbs., naturally gave more room. The valve gear remained untouched but the hopeful double exhaust valves were fitted to later engines. Between 1928 and 1932 138 new engines of this kind were built, and they eventually pottered about on secondary duties on all parts of the L.M. system. If their performance was indifferent, their simple and robust construction in relation to their usually light duties produced the lowest average repair cost in pence per mile of any of the passenger types.

The third alternative would have been to do what ex-Midlander Clayton actually did in his new abode on the S.E. & C.R. Faced with the same problem of modernising an older 4–4–0 he also replaced the cylinder block by a new design, but in this case large valves having 1½″ lap were placed on top, and the limited travel of the existing valve gear was multiplied through unequal armed rocking shafts. The result was a locomotive very similar in size and even appearance to the new L.M. engines, but the difference in their performance was as day is to night. I sometimes wonder how the latter would have fared hauling the heavy continental expresses as their counterparts did before the 'King Arthur' Class 4–6–0's became available. But I don't really wonder, I know!

In 1930, thirty more Garratts were ordered from Beyer Peacocks. They were 'improved' by the addition of double exhaust valves, and had totally enclosed rotary bunkers, to obviate the intolerable plague of coal dust blown into the cab when operating bunker first. Otherwise they were unchanged from the first three, and the whole group took over the principal Toton to Brent workings. Since one fireman had now to shovel into the firebox the same amount of coal that had formerly done on the separate double headed 0–6–0's, it is small wonder that the popularity of the Garratts amongst the men was rather dim at first. Over a ten year period these engines averaged 116.6 lbs of coal per mile.

This brings me to the last new design of any consequence produced in this era, namely the Class 7 0–8–0 Freight locomotive (Plate 28). There was traffic scope for something between the Garratts on the one hand and the Class 4 0–6–0's on the other. This gap was in fact nicely filled by the ex-L.N.W. G2 class superheated 0–8–0, by far the best Crewe design of modern times. Although made up of ingredients common to other types, they were combined in a more harmonious manner, and the generally low load factor of freight working abated many of the bad habits which higher duties called forth from their stable mates. On test they rather mystified the Derby brigade by producing marginally lower coal figures than for the Class 4 0–6–0's. Justice was restored however by their addiction to hot boxes, and an overall repair cost some 50% above that of the home product. The boiler could not be faulted, having already been re-arranged in Belpaire form under Hughes' direction. The firebox was restayed however to carry 200 lbs. per sq. in. and a redesign of the rest of the engine was now undertaken.

Once more the vacillations of this period were strongly in evidence. Now the Henderson rather than the Campbell part of the office was in the ascendancy, really first class inside cylinders were provided with plain six ring valve heads, and long lap inside Walschaert valve gear. The immediate result was a 30% reduction in coal per drawbar horsepower hour compared with the G2. Unfortunately this excellence was tragically combined with undersized bearings, the inevitable and insufficient axleboxes of the Midland Class 4 freight again being used.

In bearing area where it was wanted, and in form of construction, they were inadequate for the severe piston thrusts inherent in the inside cylinder arrangement, so that the good efficiency was quite cancelled out by the short periods the engines would run before the whole of the running gear required repair. In this respect they proved inferior in fact to the G2's which they replaced and this is the reason why they were all broken up after a relatively short life and long before the old North Western stalwarts disappeared. So here was one matter, the only one I think, in which Crewe design had the last laugh (Plate 29).

Several references have been made to efforts to improve the Claughtons, and these efforts were continued unremittingly. The work of the Derby office with improved tube ratios and spacing, was combined with the first application of the new piston valve heads in No. 5923. Twenty of these engines were fitted with new larger diameter boilers having 200 lbs. pressure of which 10 mentioned above had Caprotti gear, half of this latter group were arranged with cranks at 135° giving eight beats per revolution (Plate 30). At a later stage one of the original engines, No. 6001, was fitted with the Kylchap blast pipe and chimney as shown in Plate 32, although this modification was not continued. Finally the success of the Royal Scot inspired Derby to make the biggest change of all, consisting of retaining the enlarged Claughton boiler, and building round it what was in effect a Royal Scot 3-cylinder chassis complete. Two such engines were turned out in 1930, Nos. 5902 and 5971, retaining the L.N.W. radial bogies and old wheel centres. Notwithstanding a lower boiler pressure, they showed themselves fully equal to the Scot's in efficiency. Although this was only moderately better than was displayed by the best of the

Plate 24. G.W.R. 'Castle' class 4–6–0 No. 5000 *Launceston Castle* at Carlisle (Durran Hill) during trials on the former L.N.W. main line in 1926.

Plate 25.
The first 'Royal Scot' 4–6–0 No. 6100 leaves Crewe on trial, October 1927.

Plate 26.
General Strike, 1926; the author (left) and D. W. Sanford (right) shunting Derby Yard on Midland 2–4–0 No. 174.

Plate 27.
A Fowler 2–6–2 nears Radlett with a Moorgate-St. Albans train.

Plate 28. A Fowler class 7 0–8–0 on indicating tests in May 1930.

Plate 29. Ex-L.N.W. class G2 0–8–0 No. 49310 nears Leighton Buzzard with an up stopping freight train in August 1959.

Plate 30. L.N.W. 'Claughton' 4–6–0 No. 5927 *Sir Francis Dent* rebuilt with larger boiler and Caprotti valve gear, and seen here in L.M.S. crimson lake livery.

improved normal Claughtons, undoubted mechanical design defects of the latter were largely eliminated and repair costs averaged over an 8-year period were 50% lower.

Apart from a small group of 10 short-wheelbase 0–6–0 dock tank engines, the foregoing is the sum total of design effort under the Fowler regime, and it no doubt appears as a very reprehensible story of vacillation and ignorance of first principles of thermodynamics and of mechanics. So of course it was, but once again it is necessary to remind ourselves that in judging the past, the conditions at the time are more important than afterthought. This period represented a kind of crossroads in locomotive history. For fifty years and more design had followed a set pattern, and the insularity of the old railways withheld true knowledge of the manner in which Churchward had broken out of the charmed circle on the G.W.R. With coal as cheap as it then was, thermal efficiency loomed only faintly in the eyes of operating and motive power people. Thus, as users, and on the L.M.S. at any rate, as arbiters of what was wanted, they tended always to argue thus: "The small and medium powered engines to which we have been accustomed do their job with a minimum of repairs and trouble. Therefore in future development towards more power, the safe and reliable thing is to retain all of these well-tried features. We must beware of the Drawing Office's new-fangled ideas for more efficiency which are sure to bring us trouble, certainly at first, even if not in the long run." This view was very powerful, and where operating influences were in the ascendancy, was for a time almost mandatory. Another cross-current was management policy, which has frequently through railway history been uncertain as to the role of the engineer—that is whether he should dominate design and construction by virtue of his technical knowledge, or whether he should merely design and build to the specification of the user, i.e. the operating department. This current became positively turgid where a quasi-independent superintendent of motive power existed, himself an engineer by training. Although nominally responsible to both C.M.E. and Operating Superintendent he almost invariably inclined to the views and policies of the latter. If he had any strong views of his own on design, then he could play up a glorious Tom Tiddler's ground of conflicting interests.

Further, at that time the engineering side itself could only learn the effect of its innovations by trial and error. Recent experience with diesel traction has re-emphasised how long a period of gestation is needed for any new development on rail. Thus high degree superheat, higher boiler pressures, and improvements in valves, valve gears, and bearings had each experienced their own teething troubles. The way ahead was often obscure when it is remembered how easily a mistake could ground a whole locomotive class, or at least require expensive campaign changes of important components —matters which managements were apt to view most seriously.

And to crown all, contrary to widespread belief, locomotive design was not the only or even the most important part of the duties of a C.M.E. Because it is outside the province of this story I have said nothing of the profound reorganisation of repair methods and equipment at both Crewe and Derby works carried out in this period. The separation of engine from boiler repairs greatly reduced the time any given locomotive could spend in the workshops for periodic repairs. Repair methods and applications of new and improved materials, administration of clerical, technical and workshop staffs, and all the intricacies of financial control of a large and diverse engineering activity, were his daily diet. Chosen primarily therefore as a good departmental manager, it was fortunate rather than inevitable that a C.M.E. might also be sufficiently experienced and interested in design to assume a commanding position in that particular function.

Reverting to my own affairs, I have already told of the part I played on the production drawings for the 2–6–4 Tank, and this was, as it turned out, the last such work in the body of the office which I was to do for the remainder of my career. I was of course to make many more drawings, but all connected with testing or development in which I was henceforth to be concerned. During my days in Horwich I had had a good deal to do with the Dynamometer Car. At first in Derby I was most disgusted to find it manned by Sanford's staff, and found little solace while these people were roaming up and down the country in tests which established the optimum dimensions for the Midland compounds. They also recorded the results of various Claughton modifications, and put to the question such oddments as Caledonian 4–4–0 No. 124 between Carlisle and Leeds, and Somerset and Dorset 2–8–0 No. 88 between Toton and Brent.

The turning point came in June 1926 when due to concentration of the Testing Section staff on other jobs, I was sent out in charge of a series of tests between Preston and Carlisle with engine 14630, the first of 20 4–6–0's built for Scotland to the design of the former Caledonian '60' class, and one of the 163 non-standard engines which were built after grouping as the residue of policies initiated under the influence of the former companies or their officers. I remember these tests particularly, not only because I was for the first time in command in the field, but also because our driver was the legendary David Gibson, doyen of Caledonian enginemen, who had been associated for so many years with the famous ‘ Cardean ’. What he thought about 14630 in its red livery he kept to himself, but he had applied to smokebox door and regulator handle those embellishments in brass filigree which were a sign of the pride these old timers had in their job. By October I had become seconded to this kind of work permanently.

A Dynamometer Car is in its essentials a spring balance on wheels, plus a means of speed recording. One end of the spring is attached to the car underframe and the other end to the drawbar. With the vehicle placed between engine and train, drawbar pull and speed are measured. The earliest such cars were small 4-wheelers containing little more than the above, and they tended to be used more for train resistance experiments than for measurements of locomotive efficiency. As already mentioned the L. & Y. had a car of this kind in 1896 which Aspinall used for the subject matter of his paper on Train Resistance before the Institution of Civil Engineers in 1901.

The new Horwich car built in 1913 had the above ingredients, but the effects of pull and speed were multiplied continuously by a mechanical integrator, so that work done in horsepower hours was marked on the chart, and added up on a counter at the end of each run. This car, 50′ long, was mounted on 4-wheel bogies on one of which an additional wheel could be raised or lowered onto one rail for the establishment of speed and distance. Amenities included a raised ‘ balloon ’ front end with armchairs from where all activities on the engine footplate could be observed. There was also a large saloon in which the work table was situated, a compartment fitted out with first-class sections, a galley with coal stove, a lavatory, and rear storeroom. As on its originating railway it was only used for very short trips, it carried no steam heating equipment, no corridor connection to the rest of the train and was fitted only for gas lighting.

This vehicle provided a travelling home for a basic crew of three, the man in charge and one assistant who did the coal weighing, plus another man to ride on the footplate to take all of the necessary observations on the engine. No attendant was carried and we provided all of our own social services. If indicating was to be done, two more men were added to occupy the shelters on the front buffer beam (Plate 31). A senior locomotive inspector knowledgeable in the class of locomotive being tested was attached for each series and he looked after all the operating department obligations of the test as distinct from the technical matters which were the responsibility of the car crew. According to the importance of the test, a floating population of officials attended and rode in the car from C.M.E. and Operating Chief downwards. As the work became more routine and regular there were numerous runs made without the presence of these gentry.

To me, working these tests was a matter of great enjoyment. The intrinsic interest of the work itself, the often dramatic outcome of comparing one locomotive with another, the freedom from office routine, and the responsibility of doing a good job on one's own all combined to generate much personal satisfaction. To travel the length and breadth of the system, to enter shed life and hob-nob with railwaymen of many grades and all degrees of standing was a rewarding experience much appreciated. The purchase of food for the day's run, the cooking and tea making, the keeping of the car spick and span at all times never seemed like work, while at the end of the test, the weighing off of coal from the tender, the working out of the principal results and their dispatch to the home office completed an often hard but happy routine.

On the other hand we suffered acutely from cold when working at night with fitted freight trains. The sole source of heat was the coal-fired galley stove and one night on the way from London to Sheffield we got this stoked up to such intensity that it set the car roof smouldering. An uncomfortable time was spent by all, dousing the chimney exit with pails of water so that signal men would not see the sparks and stop the test.

Although in our travels we usually stayed in commercial hotels or when available in enginemen's barracks, sometimes it was more convenient to bed down on the seats or floor of the passenger compartment in the car. Here if one was inside the shed, the turning on of injectors or the dropping of fire-irons provided an obbligato to one's dreams, and stabled once in the open at Luton on a siding, the approach and passing of the night expresses on the adjacent main line produced nightmares of a most painful description!

Between tests and back in the office the rolls on which the various data had been inscribed were analysed, and the final reports for each test series were completed. At this time the refinements of constant speed testing were unknown to us and although the variable speed testing on normal running schedules which we carried out was not strictly accurate in itself, because it did not pay full regard to the relation between resistance of engine and resistance of train, nevertheless because the tests were made over given routes with given loads appropriate to the engine classes, and all with coal from the same colliery—the resulting comparisons were sufficient for the purposes of the day. Table 4 gives a list of the tests carried out while I was in charge and indicates the kind

Table IV. L.M.S. Dynamometer Car tests, 1926-1930 inclusive. (Author in charge)

	Date	*Engine*	*Route*	*Report No.*
1926	June	Caledonian 4–6–0 No. 14630 G.W.R.	Carlisle-Preston	7
	Nov.	"Castle" No. 5000	Crewe-Carlisle	8
1927	Oct.	Hughes 4–6–0 No. 10432 with Dabeg Pump	Manchester-Blackpool	11
	Oct./Nov.	Royal Scot 4–6–0 No. 6100	Euston-Carlisle-Glasgow	13
	Dec.	Horwich 2–6–0 Fitted Freight	Stockport-London Leeds-London	14
1928	Jan./Feb./Mar.	Garratt (first series) VS Cl. 3 & 4 0–6–0 on Coal Trains	Toton-Brent	15
	Mar./Apr.	Ljungstrom Turbine Fitted Freight	Leeds-London	16
	Mar.	L.N.E. 4–6–2's Nos. 2544 and 4473	Doncaster-Peterborough	L.N.E. Report
1929	Jan./Mar.	Royal Scot Nos. 6118, 6115, 6137, 6134, 6112. Various conditions and modifications.	Euston-Carlisle-Glasgow	19
		(Dynamometer Car given general	repair)	
	Nov./Dec.	Class 2 4–4–0 Engines with and without double exhaust valves.	Derby-Bristol	23
1930	Jan.	2–6–4T. No. 2300	St. Pancras-Luton	22
	Apr.	Wagon Resistance Tests Std. Class 7 0–8–0	Staveley Sidings	24
	May	S. & D. 2–8–0 and Std. Class 7 0–8–0	Bath-Wellow	25
	May/June	Claughton 5973 Std. and 6001—Kylala blastpipe	Leeds-Carlisle	26
	July	Hughes 4–6–0 No. 10464 Std. No. 10456 Compound	Carlisle-Preston	27
	May/June/July	Std. Class 7 0–8–0–19″ VS 19½″ dia. Cylinders Various qualities of Coal	Toton-Brent and former L. & Y. Lines	28
	July	Hughes Baltic Tank 11112 VS Std. 2–6–4T. No. 2371	Manchester to Southport and Colne	29
	Sep.	Std. Class 7 0–8–0 Further varieties of coal	Toton-Brent	30
	Oct.	Royal Scot No. 6158—Narrow Piston Valve Rings	Crewe-Carlisle	31
	Nov./Dec.	Garratt No. 4967 (Second Series)	Toton-Brent	

of information which was being sought in that era. I was mainly assisted by M. A. Henstock, who after a number of positions in Derby Works later became Assistant Stores Superintendent, Euston, and the names of Baggaley, Woore, Leam and Ellis Brown recur to my memory as partaking in these rites from time to time. The latter became in time Works Manager at Crewe and is now Locomotive Manager, BR Workshops.

In the early part of 1928 Nemesis overtook our work and our complacency was laid in the dust! It came about thus. The first series of tests with the new Royal Scot engines showed coal consumptions averaging round 2.7 lbs. of coal per drawbar horsepower, which results were published with a good deal of 'Ballyhoo'. Fowler and all of his staff, including of course myself, basked in reflected glory. Far off on the other side of England a great locomotive engineer took a long look at what his own modern engines were doing, did a few sums, and began to wonder. In due course he approached Sir Henry with compliments for his fine achievement, but went on to say that he suspected the accuracy of the old North Eastern Dynamometer Car of 1909 which was all he had to test with, and would Sir Henry be so good as to loan him the fine modern and accurate L.M.S. car. Nothing loath, our chief fell into the trap, and all of the rest of us with him, and the car was duly loaned. There it was coupled back to back with the home car and runs were made up and down the main line.

On March 22nd, 1928, Pacific No. 2544 took the combined group plus 249 trailing tons from Doncaster to Peterborough and No. 4473 brought it back with 391 tons. Plate 33 was taken during the turnround at Peterborough.

Oh calamity! The report issued a week later by T. Robson, in charge of L.N.E.R. locomotive testing, showed a discrepancy in measured drawbar pull which averaged 44% more for the L.M. car on the outward trip and 31% more on the return, the divergence being greater at the lower values—and it was not the Darlington Car which was at fault. The report comments drily: "The increased work done as shown by the L.M.S. Car of course has the effect of showing the 'Royal Scot' to be much more efficient than it really is. Our recorded observations are correct, but if it is assumed that they are wrong, and that the L.M.S. Car is correct, then our coal and water consumption figures per horsepower hour during recent trials with Pacific engines would have been reduced to such an extent as to make them impossibly low."

Thus the L.M.S. 2.7 lbs. became after correction a more realistic

3.5 lbs. per D.B.H.P. hour, indicating about the same level of efficiency which the Gresley Pacifics themselves attained at that time with higher boiler pressure and long-lap valves. There was indeed no engineering reason why the performance in this respect should have been any different.

One learns in the school lab. to calibrate one's measuring instruments, so how could it be that Hughes, the academic Billington, the Horwich staff, Sir Henry, Chambers, Sanford, B.A., the Derby staff, to say nothing of myself, all went on over the years using the Horwich car without any doubt as to its accuracy? Although it is not an excuse, there is an explanation. It is well known that when leaf springs are buckled together in the usual way with plates in contact, there is friction between them which tends to grow with time, so that the hystereris, or difference in deflection between load applied and load relieved, also increases. Had our car been fitted with a spring of this kind no doubt periodic calibration would have struck everyone as essential. But the spring actually used was not like that. Each of the 9 leaves in the 'pulling' group and 7 leaves in the 'pushing' group were mounted independently with no contact one with another, the ends of the leaves being connected by pins and links. Friction and hysteresis was therefore assumed to be negligible, and since in the protected and frequently inspected position of the springs under the car, no deterioration of the properties of the spring steel itself could be imagined, all was assumed to be permanently well.

Needless to say, on return to Derby, the car and its equipment was pulled to pieces, when there was readily seen from the top with the body off that which had not been obvious when viewed from underneath in service. While the springs themselves were all right, the whole of the system of rods and rocking lever which compensated for relative buffer and drawbar movements, and which had to move bodily in sympathy with changes in drawbar pull, was indeed the subject of very marked hysteresis. This was because the supporting rollers had seized on their pins, and the gear was in fact sliding stickily upon flats worn on the periphery of the rollers.

A complete general repair was the result and a calibrating device was designed and built which, when bolted temporarily onto the headstocks before each series of tests, enabled the effect of deadweights loaded onto the scale pan to be measured in drawbar pen deflection, ton for ton. At the same time a number of improved amenities were provided in the car body, such as steam heating, electric light, and a gangway connection at the rear end. With a coat of L.M.S. red the car finally appeared as shown in Plate 34, and rendered many years of useful and accurate service thereafter. These improvements greatly eased the lot of the staff who felt, for a time at any rate, that it did not really deserve such a reward!

Long after, in Stanier's time, and as a result of some leg-pulling between the two chiefs, a replay was arranged. Once again the two cars were coupled back to back and in November 1934, a further round trip was made, this time between Darlington and York. The difference was now recorded as less than 1% and a laconic note from Gresley said: "I do not want any further data. The results of the tests show that the two cars are for all practical purposes alike."

Table V. New steam locomotives added to L.M.S. stock during four years, 1926-1930 (inc.)

			1926	*1927*	*1928*	*1929*	*1930*	*Total*
Standard Designs								
Class 6	4-6-0	3 cyl. Royal Scot	—	50	—	20	—	70
Class 5X	4-6-0	3 cyl. (Parallel Boiler)	—	—	—	2	—	2
Class 4	4-4-0	3 cyl. Compound	5	50	—	—	—	55
Class 2	4-4-0	2 cyl.	—	—	50	19	4	73
Class 4	2-6-4	'Fowler' Tank	—	4	21	50	—	75
Class 3	2-6-2	'Fowler' Tank	—	—	—	—	21	21
Class 7	0-8-0	Freight Tender	—	—	—	100	3	103
Class 5	2-6-0	Horwich Mixed Traffic	13	87	8	22	95	225
Class 4	0-6-0	Supr. Freight	132	137	89	—	—	358
	2-6-6	2 Garratt	—	3	—	—	30	33
Class 3	0-6-0	Freight Tank	128	36	157	36	—	357
Class 2	0-6-0	Dock Tank	—	—	7	3	—	10
			278	367	332	252	153	1382
Existing Non-Standard Designs Perpetuated								
Class 4	4-6-0	Caledonian 14530 class	18	—	—	—	—	18
Class 3	4-4-2	'Tilbury' Tank	—	10	—	—	10	20
			18	10	—	—	10	38

IV

Interregnum

1931

ON Saturday morning, January 10th, 1931, I was, without prior warning, summoned up to Chambers's office and into the presence of E. J. H. Lemon. In very few words I was instructed to start at Euston on Monday morning and to make arrangements accordingly. Appointments were then often made in this sudden manner, without any of the paraphernalia of advertisement, applications, interviews, etc. One found out afterwards what rise was attached, which seldom exceeded £50. The event signalled the end of Sir Henry Fowler's reign, and the entering into office, as the new C.M.E., of Ernest Lemon who, up to then, had been in charge of the Carriage and Wagon side of the department. Fowler did not retire there and then, but continued for some time longer as a scientific and research adviser to the management, without real power, and thus passed into a twilight in which he no longer even nominally controlled our actions.

Lemon was a very different kind of person from his predecessor, short, dark, abrupt and exceedingly experienced and competent in all aspects of production and administration. Even during his late incumbency he had continued the rationalisation of carriage and wagon production and maintenance begun by his illustrious predecessor, R. W. Reid. Of locomotives he was largely ignorant, but he was presumably appointed not to dwell upon the niceties of design, but to put some fire into the overall business side of the department, and to drive through real economies. His office was to be at Euston, in the closest touch with the management, and there he set up a small technical headquarters, consisting of two main sections. S. J. Symes, at one time Derby Locomotive Works Manager, and currently Locomotive Assistant, continued to look after the locomotive side, with a squad which now included myself. The other small section was under T. Hornbuckle, a personal friend of Lemon's from his previous office, who was something of an original thinker and who was used mainly for development work on the non-steam and rolling stock side. The chief naturally continued to control Carriage & Wagon matters himself with the redoubtable assistance of John Purves who transferred from Wolverton to Derby. H. P. M. Beames now moved over from Crewe to Derby as Deputy C.M.E., and thus enters once more upon the scene as poacher turned gamekeeper. During the next twelve months of Lemon's tenure as C.M.E. it was pull devil pull baker between Symes and Beames as regards the locomotive design policy which should be followed, with no strong lead available from the new chief on a subject so unfamiliar to him.

Symes was a delightful person, unruffled, and courteous. He had been Chief Draughtsman at Derby before Chambers and his knowledge of, and interest in, design, was profound. He only lacked strong convictions as to the direction new design should take, and preferred to let it evolve as a result of carefully accumulated facts regarding the existing types. Thus, after a period of ruthless Midlandisation, the pendulum swung towards the earlier trend of trying to establish merit and to select the best. In this he tended to be thwarted somewhat by Beames who, if not technically senior, was at least co-equal in his call upon Lemon's ear, and who was adamantine in his belief that everything Crewe was best.

Thus, in place of crossing the lattice foot bridge to work at Derby, I now approached my new office through the profundities of the Euston Great Hall, past the huge statue of George Stephenson, and up the cascading steps through the mighty columns which led towards the holy places of High Direction and Management. Alas, the glory soon diminished. The C.M.E. had an office on the entrance floor, but the rest of us, two flights up, inhabited low sombre rabbit hutches looking on to the eaves and blank walls of the station itself, haunts of London pigeons and sparrows disporting themselves on generous carpets of soot and smokebox char.

Although still designated 'Draughtsman' my job was now to go out on to the line, on the footplate and in the sheds to assemble the facts regarding particular engine classes, and then in the office, to work up proposals for modification or new design resulting therefrom. These proposals would be passed on to the principal Drawing Offices. On the first part of this remit I was teamed up with 'Bill' Bramley of the Motive Power H.Q. Staff under Anderson. Together we stumped the country, visiting sheds, examining repair cards, and seeing with our own eyes the results in service of all kinds of design matters from leaky smokebox doors all the way through to defective tender sump sieves. This was my first direct contact with 'motive power' work, and it was a liberal education in cause and effect, with a certain element of crime detection for good measure. This work was the forerunner of the mechanical inspectors' section subsequently much expanded by Stanier and Ivatt.

The railway now had 380 fully satisfactory modern locomotives of recent construction, Royal Scots, 2–6–4 Tanks and 2–6–0 Mixed Traffics, these out of a total of 8,450 engines. The second eleven, as it were, a total of 1,132 engines consisting of Claughtons, Hughes 4–6–0's, Prince of Wales, George V's, 0–8–0's of both L.N.W. and Standard designs, had still to undertake a large volume of important traffic, and the passage of time did not make them any more ideally suitable for these duties than has already been described. The large numbers of the purely Midland designs were all of smaller capacity, and while they leavened the mass of other regional types in low repair costs their work was less efficient and made little contribution towards the heavier duties. Thus the activities of our new office at Euston was largely concentrated upon the above mentioned second string. When Lemon passed on to higher office, after only 12 months' tenure of the post of C.M.E., proposals had already been evolved as to what to do in each case.

The first target was the 'Claughtons'. Putting to sea in a sieve was as nothing compared to the problem of how to put these engines to rights! As already mentioned they were now being fitted with new piston valve heads having six rings each, which greatly improved their coal consumption. However, mechanically they were getting ten times more hot boxes pro rata than the Royal Scots, and demanding ten times more maintenance cost on rods and motion. Any improvement in the entry of oil into the axleboxes was negatived by a clearance of only $1\frac{7}{8}''$ between firebox foundation ring and axlebox top. This distance was further reduced while running due to spring flexure. Their vacuum brake system required three times the maintenance of the Midland version, and there were excessive repair costs due to smokebox doors, sanding, loose cabs and splashes and broken springs. Even the buffer bodies were weak and broke like carrots on the kind of impacts common in shed yards. Over a trial period of 54 days, 6.7% of the Scots were found stopped for defects or repairs, while 27% of the original Claughtons were immobilised for the same reason. In considering repair expenditure, at 4.7d. per mile for the former, and 7d. per per mile for the latter, the level of costs of those days must be remembered.

The 10 engines which had been fitted with larger boilers and regraded Class 5X were little better, while the 10 other engines rebulit with Caprotti valve gear produced the same volume of trouble in the same time. Because of Beames' special interest in them they were kept on high mileage jobs, with the result that both failures and repair costs per mile were somewhat less.

However much Beames wished to save the Claughton in recognisable form, and notwithstanding all that the Caprotti gear could contribute, the facts which were brought to light were incontrovertible. A recommendation was made in October and accepted by the Board, that 20 of this class falling due for new cylinders and boilers in 1932 should be 'rebuilt' to the same 3-cylinder design as the two prototype engines referred to in the last chapter. In other words they should be scrapped and replaced. Thus was pronounced the death knell of this controversial class.

The 'Prince of Wales' was next examined and, apart from an even more appalling record of hot boxes, it was plagued with broken frames as already described. Beyond this it had all the lesser ills to which the Claughton was subject. Titbits from its record were 23 engines at one shed which consumed 250 coil-bearing springs in 12 months, and Joy's valve gear die blocks which required remetalling every 20,000 miles.

It was now that Beames asserted himself and he was able to persuade Lemon that all of these difficulties could be overcome. For future new locomotives for comparable duties a modified Prince of Wales design was therefore evolved as shown in Fig. 11. Caprotti valve gear was the centrepiece, and axlebox trouble was to be avoided by the application of mechanical lubrication—made possible by raising the boiler centre-line, to give adequate free space between axlebox tops and foundation ring. A simple running board and rudimentary cab got rid of the troublesome splashers, and a moderate application of Midland features such as brake equipment, steam sanding and more robust mechanical details were to complete the transformation. Symes, having won the day over the Claughton conversion, was not in this case inclined to develop a counter proposal. However, he was uneasy, as were all of us on his staff, that there was something wrong somewhere with the thinking which produced this effort. None the less, this is what would undoubtedly have been built as the leading mixed traffic class, had Stanier not come along in good time with quite other ideas. The real snag in the design was that the heavy longitudinal thrusts from the inside cylinders remained, with the

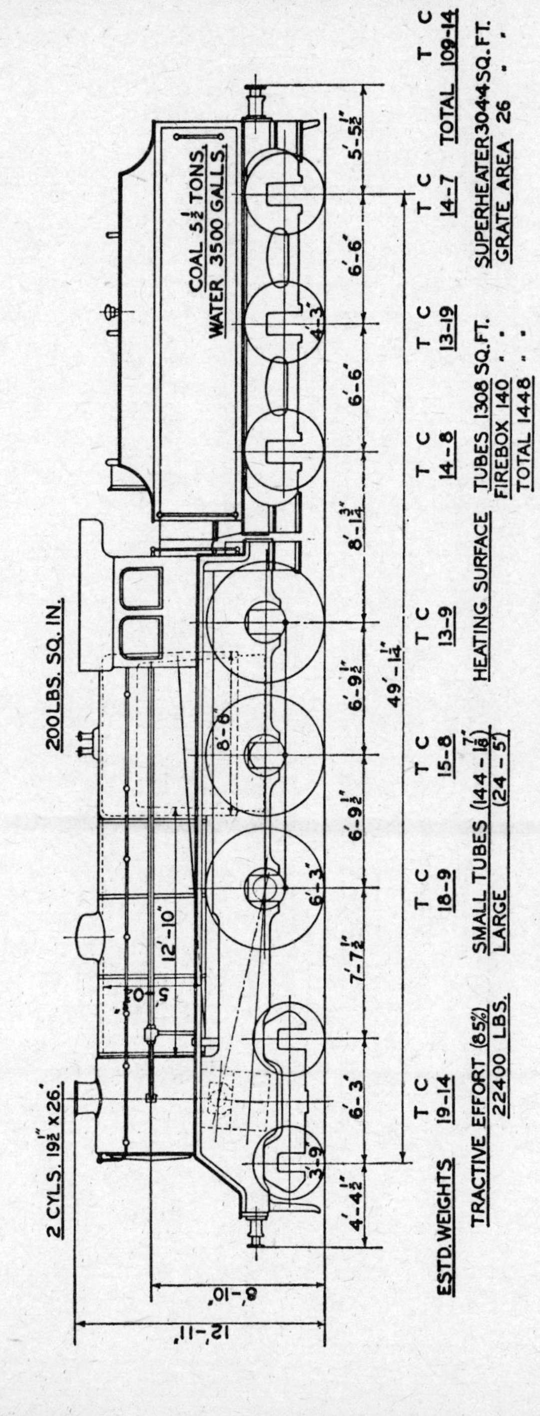

MODERNISED 4-6-0 PRINCE OF WALES DESIGN – 1931.

Fig. 11

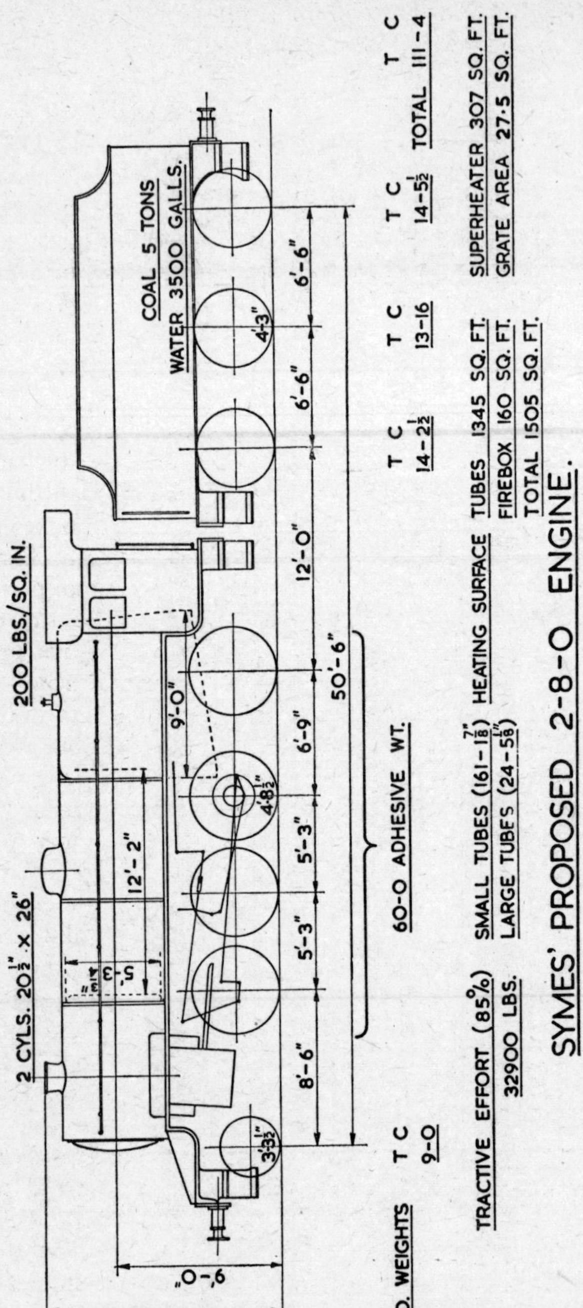
2 CYLS. 20½" x 26"
200 LBS./SQ. IN.
COAL 5 TONS
WATER 3500 GALLS.
12'-10½"
9'-0"
3'-3½"
4'-8½"
4'-3"
5'-3⅛"
12'-2"
9'-0"
8'-6"
5'-3"
5'-3"
6'-9"
12'-0"
6'-6"
6'-6"
50'-6"
60-0 ADHESIVE WT.
ESTD. WEIGHTS
T C 9-0
T C 14-2½
T C 13-16
T C 14-5½
T C TOTAL 111-4
TRACTIVE EFFORT (85%) 32900 LBS.
SMALL TUBES (161-1⅞") LARGE TUBES (24-5⅛")
HEATING SURFACE TUBES 1345 SQ. FT. FIREBOX 160 SQ. FT. TOTAL 1505 SQ. FT.
SUPERHEATER 307 SQ. FT.
GRATE AREA 27·5 SQ. FT.
SYMES' PROPOSED 2-8-0 ENGINE.

Fig. 12

axleboxes unchanged to mitigate their effects. Hot boxes and early deterioration would have continued as before despite mechanical lubrication.

As regards the eight coupled freight engine group, detailed investigations were made into the ex-L.N.W. G_1 and G_2 classes, 401 and 60 strong respectively. Also studied were the 120 new class 7 Standard engines then running and finally the Somerset & Dorset 2–8–0's. Although only eleven of the latter existed they were the quintessence of Derby practice, according to the Fowler/Anderson school. As already mentioned, the North Western types were the best of their kind but nobody, not even Beames, wanted to build more of this old design. The standard 7's were already a sad disappointment, due to their being undershod, and in 1930 alone the 120 engines had generated 53 hot coupled boxes. Moreover, 4 flawed and one broken crank axle had already had to be replaced. The S. & D. engine, since also equipped with the famous Class 4 freight axleboxes gave a like record of hot boxes in proportion, but in all other respects was mechanically first class. Only its cylinders obstinately remained too wide to permit the required general route availability. Thus none of the existing types merited further construction and three alternative proposals were developed, one from Euston and two from Derby. Symes, following his wish to select the best, now caused me to outline the layout shown in Fig. 12 which produced a straightforward 2–8–0 having a number of well-tried components such as the Horwich 2–6–0 boiler and cylinder castings. There is little reason to think that this would not have produced a very satisfactory machine had it been built. At Derby Beames directed development towards an outside cylinder version of the Class 7 in 2–8–0 form, using the same boiler. This is shown in Fig. 13. He also produced something more massive, in the form of a 4–8–0, having the enlarged Claughton boiler as shown in Fig. 14. Lemon was quite unable to make a selection between these alternatives. Despite their defects 15 more of the existing Class 7 0–8–0's were put on the 1932 building programme, and the problem was shelved for the time being.

While all this activity was proceeding the drawing offices were not entirely inactive, although in some of them the old practice of working out small alteration jobs over and over again must have been resumed. Two partially new designs were in fact produced during the year, and turned out in 1932. The first of these, a 0–4–4 tank was a triumph for the forces of reaction. There was

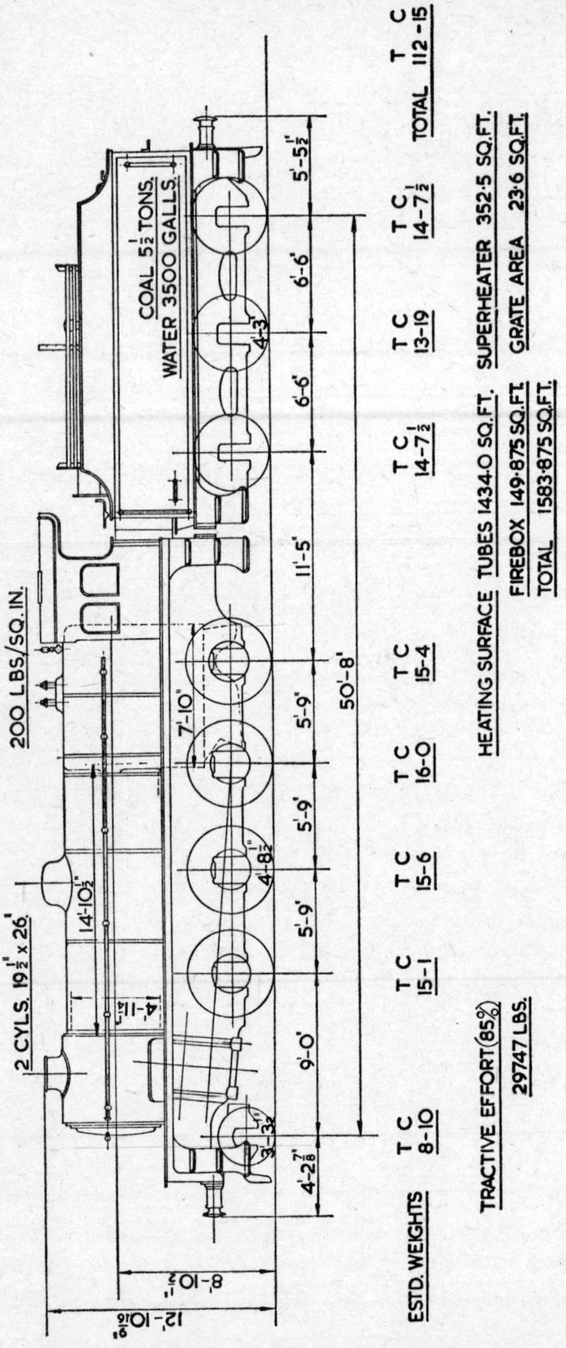

BEAMES' PROPOSED 2-8-0 FREIGHT ENGINE.

Fig. 13

Plate 31. Indicating the Fowler 0–8–0.

Plate 32. Small boilered 'Claughton' 4–6–0 No. 6001 fitted with 'Kylchap' blast pipe and wider chimney; the engine is seen here coupled to a G.C. type tender from a withdrawn R.O.D. 2–8–0.

Plate 33. Gresley Pacific No. 4473 at Peterborough with the Horwich Dynamometer Car on March 22nd, 1928.

Plate 34. The Horwich Dynamometer Car, as rebuilt in 1929.

Plate 35. The Beyer, Peacock Lungström turbine condensing locomotive leaves St. Pancras with a Manchester express.

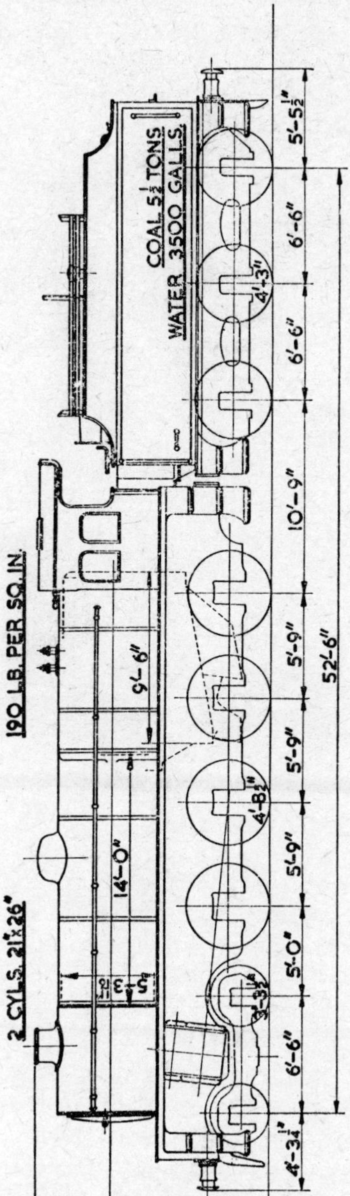

ESTD. WEIGHTS	T C	T C	T C	T C	T C	T C	T C	T C	T C
	19–5	15–7	16–1	15–11	15–6	14–7½	13–19	14–7½	TOTAL 124–4

TRACTIVE EFFORT (85%) 32775 LB.

SMALL TUBES (140–2⅛")
LARGE TUBES (24–5¼")

HEATING SURFACE TUBES 1550·0 SQ. FT.
FIREBOX 183·0 SQ. FT.
TOTAL 1733·0 SQ. FT.

SUPERHEATER 365·0 SQ. FT.
GRATE AREA 30·5 SQ. FT.

BEAMES' PROPOSED 4–8–0 FREIGHT ENGINE

Fig. 14

operating scope for a general purpose Class 2 engine of unlimited route availability—years later this need was satisfactorily fulfilled by the Ivatt 2–6–2 tanks. Now, however, Anderson, abetted by Harold Rudguard, an up and coming key motive power influence on the Midland division, demanded a replica of the Johnson design, the bulk of which had been built during the previous century. Once again, if a 0–4–4 was really the only solution, there was a more modern version already designed and in being on the North Stafford. Since only 10 were required what more simple than to build to the Stoke drawings? But no, the Midland mystique must have its fling—a final one as it turned out—and the drawing office was solemnly set to dressing up this ancient design with different smokebox, cab, tanks and trailing bogie, all of which contributed nothing at all to performance. However, there was one shattering break with past tradition, the engine was turned out with a stovepipe chimney! We all seemed to have become stovepipe minded about this time, as will be seen from the diagram of current proposals already mentioned. I think this must be ascribed to Beames' influence, which overlapped into the early stages of Stanier's design work. Although a trifle, of not the slightest technical importance, there is hardly any feature which so determines the whole nature of a steam locomotive's appearance as the shape of the chimney top.

The other design was to meet a need for five more 'Jinties', that is 0–4–0 saddle tanks suitable for docks, brewery sidings and so on. Once more a good deal of redesign was undertaken on the theme of the previous small batch of similar Midland engines, but it is extremely doubtful whether the changes made were worth anything.

Apart from complete locomotives there were a number of useful development activities during the year. Authority was sought and obtained to fit nearly 1,600 engines with the 6-ring piston valves, now proved to be so effective against internal steam leakage. Bogie brakes, a true Midland feature, were found to be more trouble than they were worth and their removal was undertaken with thankfulness. A further scheme was approved for fitting 1,242 older engines with exhaust steam injectors. Although on the longer test runs this device indicated a coal saving of around 8%, on secondary duties with numerous stops this could dwindle to next to nothing. I am afraid this action was more a gesture towards economy, than any real contribution to net revenue, at any rate on a majority of the engines now fitted retrospectively.

The Royal Scots continued as the mainstay of all the important express services. Once the piston valve trouble had been solved they gave a good account of themselves, and at a lower specific cost in fuel and maintenance performed much better on comparable duties than anything else on the railway at that time. After four years, however, the onset of bad riding could no longer be ignored, and a lot of investigation was undertaken. What was happening was plain enough. Although of generous proportions, the axle-boxes followed the Midland principle of employing manganese bronze castings for the body of the box, which were considered to promote better heat transfer and dissipation than did steel. As this was not itself a bearing metal, brass strips were dovetailed into the box which when bridged by white metal, formed a composite bearing area which rode upon the axle journal. These strips even if carefully fitted into their grooves and pegged, tended to come loose and disturb the white metal. With the small inside collars which were usually turned on the axles this was particularly likely to happen, and with a big engine having heavy side thrusts disintegration was inevitable. The bad riding due to excessive lateral wear came first, and many is the wild ride I had in consequence. Then, as the whole bulk of the axleboxes lost the firmness of new construction, and repair procedure proved unable to regain it, the hot boxes started. The class which had been so good in this respect for its first years ran 25 hot coupled boxes in 1930, and by 1932 this had increased to 102, for the 70 engines. With our eyes too near the ground, palliatives were sought such as increasing the size of the axle collars, and staying the frames at the back end, but the really decisive cure did not come until the next era.

Enough has been said to display the continuing results of lack of a strong and purposeful central direction in design matters. The effects of this were accentuated by a continuing loyalty to a variety of practices which were already becoming outmoded. However, the old insularity was gradually dissolving and as part of the Royal Scot investigation I was sent, in November, on to the Southern Railway to ride the Lord Nelsons. It was now that I was able to meet Clayton and Holcroft who, sharing the same office at Waterloo, had so great an influence upon the trend of design on that region. Although these engines rode much better I am afraid that the expedition threw little light upon our own particular trouble.

It is perhaps now convenient in this pause between what was, and what was to come in locomotive policy, to refer briefly to various attempts to break away from convention in steam practice and to describe the first faint glimmerings of the dawn of diesel traction—eventually to burst into blazing noon. No signs of life were apparent on the electrification front, which after the events outlined in Chapter II, remained sunk in lethargy.

The form of the steam locomotive in Stephensonian shape was by now 100 years old. The possibility of some wholesale change was ever present in Railway Board rooms wishful of reduction in traction costs, and in the minds of outside manufacturing firms who hoped to be able to cash in on revolutionary developments. Higher thermal efficiency totally enclosed prime movers, and absence of external smoke and steam were the goals. Countless projects were put forward. Those which were built and ran have been the subject of detailed individual description and collective commentary[1,2] which the following notes amplify to some extent.

The first comprehensive effort in this country was the Reid-Ramsay Turbine Condensing locomotive, built in 1910 as a venture by the North British Loco. Co. and run for short distances on the Caledonian and North British Railways. When this was illustrated in the daily papers I well remember my annoyance when my father said that this must mean the early demise of the normal type, in which I took so much interest. My childish instinct that such could not be the case turned out to be true, and I was little to know that 27 years later I would myself be associated with the very last attempt to work out a solution along these lines. In between there were many chastening experiences, both at first and second hand.

Soon after the First World War another private venture was launched by the Ramsay Locomotive Co., which had built by Armstrong, Whitworth & Co., a new turbine electric condensing locomotive of 2–6–0, 0–6–2 wheel arrangement. The old L.N.W.R. had promised to give the company facilities for trial running and after the formation of the larger L.N.W. this promise was honoured and the engine was sent to Horwich in February 1922. It was much in evidence at that centre until it was broken up some two years later, and I witnessed with solemnity the cutting up of its frames, turbine, generator, etc., into chunks of metal destined for the scrap merchant. At 156 tons total it exceeded its estimated weight by 17 tons, and 24 tons on three out ot the six coupled axles reduced its range of action to the line between Horwich and

[1] "Recent Developments in Locomotive Design"—Presidential Address by W. A. Stanier (*Proc.* Inst. Loco. Engrs. Jnl. 133, 1936).

[2] "Years of Transition"—Presidential Address by R. C. Bond (*Proc.* Inst. Engrs. Jnl. 234, 1953).

Bolton, with one or two specially permitted forays down to Southport. This ill-starred locomotive had been designed and built without any user collaboration, and none of the numerous subsequent alterations succeeded in producing good combustion or steaming. Its maximum and final performance was to average 38 m.p.h. from Southport to Wigan with a train load of 170 tons, the hectic maximum of 50 m.p.h. being attained en route.

The next and last new construction of a condensing locomotive in this country was another venture by a private manufacturer which was altogether better founded, and only missed acceptance by a comparatively narrow margin. As early as 1922 worldwide interest had been aroused by the construction of such a locomotive in Sweden, using a Ljungström turbine, driving six coupled wheels directly through gears. The boiler, with its coal and water, was assembled on a non-driving unit, and the air-cooled condenser, mounted behind the turbine and above the coupled wheels formed the second unit. Billington had travelled to Sweden to inspect this engine in 1923, and in the latter half of the same year Messrs. Beyer Peacock obtained a provisional licence for the manufacturing rights. The firm decided to take the risk and build a locomotive of this kind suitable for British conditions. After preliminary tests in the works yard the completed engine made its first trial from Gorton to Woodhead on the L.N.E.R. on July 4th, 1926. Fowler had already agreed to give facilities for thorough trials on the L.M.S. in service conditions, and the engine left Gorton for Derby in September. Thereafter it ran slow and semi-fast trains to Manchester until the end of the year, and undertook express passenger service to London and on the Bristol line, during 1927 and 1928 (Plate 35). The whole design was neat and compact, the main features being a working pressure of 300 lbs. per sq. in., a turbine of 2,000 h.p. and 10,000 r.p.m. driving directly through treble reduction gearing and siderods, coupled wheels 5′ 3″ in diameter with a maximum axle loading of 18¼ tons. The weight of the complete locomotive was 143½ tons. Although not without its teething troubles it was capable of good performance with loads up to 400 tons passenger and 750 tons freight, thus surpassing what the Midland compound could do and foreshadowing the performance of the various 4–6–0 engines which were introduced on to the Midland lines in later years. My association with it was in the course of Dynamometer Car trials carried out in the spring of 1928 between Sheffield and London, with around 470 trailing tons of covered vans at average speeds of 36 m.p.h. A Horwich 2–6–0 also took part in the same trials for comparative purposes. The Turbine engine averaged 3.28 lbs. of coal per D.B.H.P. hour, 4% more than the reciprocating engine. Since the whole of the exhaust steam was condensed only make up for brake ejector and leakage was theoretically required, and a saving of 84% in water consumption was actually obtained compared with the conventional locomotive.

One of the features of the Ljungström engine was the delivery of heated air for combustion to the ashpan. Heated air was passed from the smokebox through ducting in which was situated a flap-shaped damper, by which the quantity of air passing could be controlled. One night in Doveholes tunnel, while mounting the 1 in 100 gradient, a pin dropped out of the control rodding so that the damper fell shut. The resulting production of dense smoke nearly asphyxiated all concerned! Although this engine was capable of doing a good job, it retained one of the basic faults which has stifled nearly every attempt at turbine condensing engines. As the boiler size was related to the steam demand at the designed condenser vacuum if for any reason the vacuum fell, boiler demand rose, and the small boiler lost efficiency in trying to meet it with a double debit to the overall coal consumption. It was finally decided that, related to its probable cost, even in quantity production, it gave no promise of economic advantage. The locomotive was returned to its makers, where it stood for a long time in the hope of interesting overseas railways in waterless terrain.

The only other attempt at the unconventional steam engine with which the L.M.S. was associated up to this time, was the application of the German Schmidt-Henschel boiler to a 'Royal Scot' built by the N.B. Loco. Co. Inc. The project was sponsored in this country by the Superheater Co. Fully described in the technical press the marvel in looking back is that anyone thought that so complex an assembly of what was virtually three boilers in the space of one, could be made to work. Even if it did, the feeding of steam at 900 lbs. per sq. in. pressure to a normal type of reciprocating cylinder was bound to produce lubrication and wear problems of some magnitude. Nevertheless the concept had appealed to a wider field and similar boilers, in addition to the original German one, were fitted to locomotives in France and Canada. Alas, in the first three weeks, while the engine was still running its first trials adjacent to the Glasgow works, one of the vertical tubes lining the firebox side overheated and burst, due to defective natural water circulation, killing an inspector. This ill-omened beginning was followed by much investigation and partial rebuilding of the boiler, so that the machine could eventually be brought to Derby, and testing continued. It was never entered into revenue service, however, because the boiler feed arrangements, having to deliver against so high a pressure, never permitted a reliable water level to be maintained. After a long period of idleness it made one last demonstration run after Stanier's advent, with no greater success. The chassis was eventually used as the basis of the first tapered boiler Royal Scot, No. 6170, turned out in 1935.

Reference has been made to the 'Garratt' locomotive which, although not forsaking the basic concept of the normal locomotive, rearranged its well-tried components in a new kind of assembly, and released it from some of its more severe limitations. Boiler diameter, depth and width of firebox, free entry of air to the grate, ample ashpan capacity were far less inhibited by loading gauge and presence of coupled wheels. Four cylinders were obtainable without crank axles, and a weight distribution was possible very favourable to route availability.

Although only two Garratt types were ever acquired by L.M.S. or B.R. the possibility of wider use was examined at intervals from 1924 to 1949, now at the behest of the railway, now at the instance of Messrs. Beyer Peacock. As it was never contested that this kind of locomotive could do a thoroughly good job, if correctly designed, the problem was always where could it be economically employed. It was necessary to bear in mind that a conventional engine was lighter and cheaper, so long as it could do the work within existing limitations.

The obvious application was where regular double heading was in use, as between Toton and Brent. It was little short of a tragedy that, at a time when design progress could have already assured much improved efficiency and freedom from bearing troubles, an engine was put on the line which contributed to neither.

This was one of the worst and last examples of a slavish adherence to outmoded practice on the part of the railway so far as locomotive design was concerned. It was certainly not the fault of the firm, who suffered not only loss of a shop window to show to its overseas visitors what the Garratt principle could really mean, but also the existence of a shadow over all its subsequent efforts to solicit further applications on British Railways.

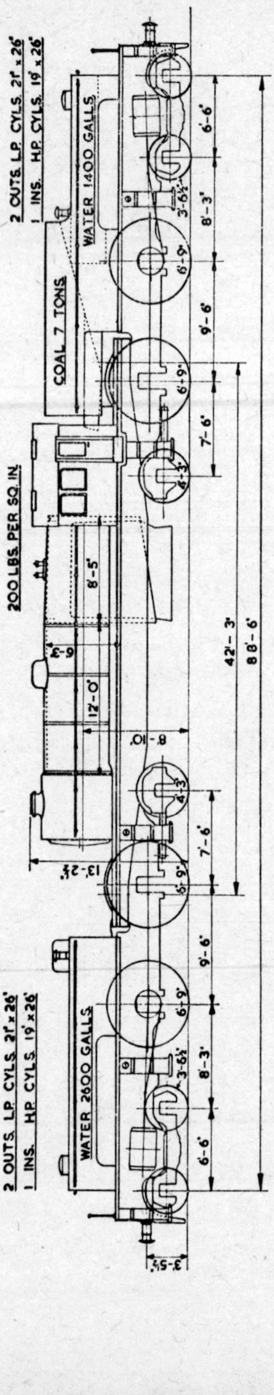

ESTD. WEIGHTS	T C	T C	T C	T C	T C	T C	T C	T C	
	27-0	21-0	21-0	16-0	16-0	21-0	21-0	27-0	TOTAL 170-0

TRACTIVE EFFORT (80%)
45,300 LBS.

SMALL TUBES (209-2")
LARGE TUBES (36-5⅛")

HEATING SURFACE TUBES 1954·0 SQ. FT.
FIREBOX 183·0 SQ. FT.
TOTAL 2137·0 SQ. FT.

SUPERHEATER 500·0 SQ. FT.
GRATE AREA 44·5 SQ. FT.

4-4-2 GARRATT 3 CYL. COMPOUND.

Fig. 15

Apart from the Midland coal trains there were two other kinds of traffic in which the Garratt might offer some advantage, namely a maximum power express passenger engine for main line service, and a mixed traffic engine for service on the Highland line. Although defeated by the facts of life, in his wish to run the Anglo-Scottish traffic by the Midland Compound alone, Anderson still hankered after his brain child. In 1930 when the 'Royal Scot' was passing through its troublesome phase, he approached the firm again with an idea for a 'Midland Compound Garratt', and this was worked out as shown in Fig. 15. At the same time the firm amplified this to indicate how a Pacific Compound Garratt would work out (Fig. 16). Both of these proposals were re-presented to Stanier in 1932 after Anderson had gone, and this time four and six cylinder simple expansion alternatives were offered. The chief was not impressed, as no Anglo-Scottish traffic was visualised at the time beyond the capacity of the Pacific currently under design.

To round off the story, although it reaches forward to a later part of this narrative, a last effort by the firm was made at the time of Nationalisation. In June 1948, and again in October 1949, a light 'Pacific' Garratt design was worked out (Fig. 17) with and without mechanical stoker, which could save double heading north of Perth. This idea of a Scottish Garratt had been germinating over a period, and at one time it had been intended to send one of the existing engines up north for trials. Unfortunately there was only one train, the 'Royal Highlander' with its sleeping cars, which called for regular double heading even with Class 5 4–6–0's, and all of the rest of the traffic could be coped with for nine months in the year by one of these engines per train. The utilisation of a big Garratt was therefore very marginal, and it was found impossible to justify it. Concurrently a modified version of this engine, having 5′ 0″ diameter wheels and every modern feature, which had by now made this kind of machine so successful overseas, was offered in replacement of the original Toton-Brent Garratts, which were falling far short of the required maintenance standard. However, with the traffic satisfactorily organised, on train loads within the capacity of single-handed 2–8–0's, the scope for savings was much diminished, and the proposal was not taken up. Table VI charts the different stages in this saga of a lost cause.

Of the diesel there is very little to record over the years up to 1931. Diagrams were prepared at Horwich in 1923 for the application of petrol engines to simple lightweight 4-wheeled vehicles, but experiments elsewhere of road buses on flanged wheels had

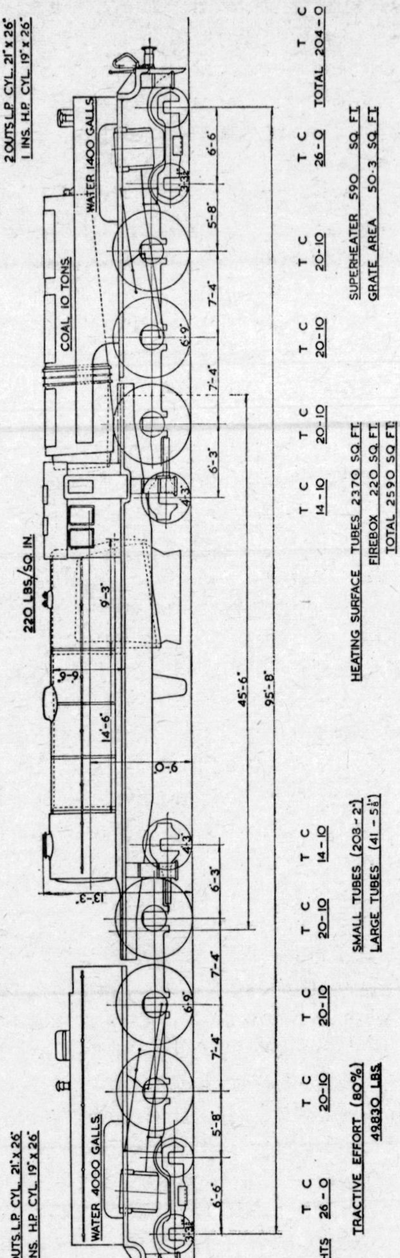

4-6-2 GARRATT 3 CYL. COMPOUND.

Fig. 16

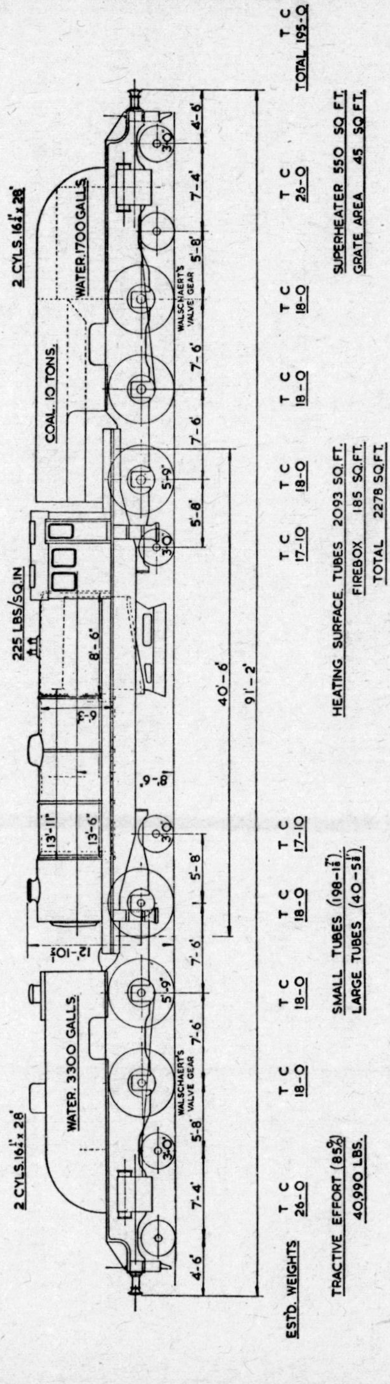

4-6-2 GARRATT FOR SCOTTISH LINES

Fig. 17

Table VI. Development of Garratt locomotives (1924-1949) for L.M.S.

Beyer Peacock Drg. No.	*Date*	*Wheel Arrangement of each Unit*	*Cylinders on each Unit*	*Coupled Wheels Dia.*	*Boiler Pressure lbs./per in.*	*Tractive Effort lbs.*	*Maximum Axle Load T. C.*	*Total Engine Weight T. C.*	*Comments*	*Fig. No.*
95866	5/24	2–6–2	$18\frac{1}{2} \times 26$	5′ 1″	180	44640	16.10	145.0	Hughes proposal (For Toton-Brent Traffic)	
98092	5/24	2–6–0	$18\frac{1}{2} \times 26$	5′ 3″	180	43220	18.10	141.0	Anderson proposal (For Toton-Brent Traffic)	
109922	4/30	4–4–2	HP 19, LP 21 × 26	6′ 9″	200	45300	21. 0	170.0	Based on Midland Compound	Fig. 15
112647	9/32	4–4–2	(3) 16 × 26	6′ 9″	225	47140	22. 0	181.0	Three Cylinder simple version	
112648	9/32	4–4–2	(2) $19\frac{1}{2}$ × 26	6′ 9″	225	46680	21. 0	176.0	Two Cylinder simple version	
109680	4/30	4–6–2	HP 19, LP 21 × 26	6′ 9″	220	49830	20. 0	200.0	More powerful version of above	Fig. 16
127114A	6/48	4–6–2	(2) $16\frac{1}{4} \times 28$	5′ 9″	225	40990	18. 0	195.0	With Stoker for Highland Lines	Fig. 17
127802	10/49	4–6–2	(2) $16\frac{1}{4} \times 28$	5′ 0″	225	47140	19. 0	193.0	With Stoker for Toton-Brent Coal Traffic	

proved unsatisfactory. Nothing was actually done until 1927 when an offer was accepted from Beardmore's to supply, for trial in rail traction, one of the diesel engines they had developed for airship propulsion. The 500 h.p. engine was both high in speed (900 r.p.m.) and light in weight ($14\frac{1}{2}$ lbs. per h.p.) for its time. English Electric transmission was used. The train consisted of four coaches converted from some spare units for the wide L. & Y. type electric stock, referred to earlier. The 1,090 lbs. per seated passenger, inclusive of motive power, was creditable by modern standards, but the power to weight ratio, $3\frac{1}{2}$ h.p. per ton, was too low and acceleration was poor. The train ran in the Blackpool area for nine months and for three August weeks of that time I stood in for the regular observer. There was a good deal to observe, for the unfortunate engine, not tractionised, and mounted in the underframe in a manner which twisted the crankcase, was out of traffic for 68% of possible working days. Quite a number of all-night sessions were spent on repairing this and replacing that. Potential comparative all-in costs, one-man operation notwithstanding, came out at 19d. per mile, as against 14d. for steam push and pull which was tried out in parallel.

It would have required extraordinary faith and prescience to have persevered, and the power unit was returned to the makers and the train broken up.

In July 1931 I attended a demonstration which, as is so often the case in railway work, had delayed-action consequences. A railcar chassis was demonstrated by a subsidiary of the A.E.C. Company at Slough, having an A.E.C. bus-type engine and 4-speed gearbox transmission. Although a petrol engine and single plate clutch were featured this was the true progenitor of that development which, expanded into a bogie vehicle and fitted with diesel engine, fluid flywheel and epicyclic gears, eventually grew into the well-known G.W.R. railcar fleet, and finally and by devious means into the British Railways fleet of 4,000 vehicles under British United Traction sponsorship. It took 25 years hard slogging and a massive contribution from Leyland Motors and A.E.C. before this development won its place in the sun.

Also in this period, which included the years of the great depression, attention was directed towards reducing shunting costs by the introduction of one-man operation, for which the diesel was specially suited. Hornbuckle commenced work towards proposals for a trial on the L.M.S. of the various makers of Diesel Shunter which were already commercially developed. This did not mature, however, until the time covered by the next two chapters.

Table VII. New steam locomotives added to L.M.S. stock during 1931.

Standard Designs

Class 2 4-4-0	2 cyl.	30
Class 3 2-6-2	'Fowler' Tank	39
Class 7 0-8-0	Freight Tender	32
Class 5 2-6-0	Horwich Mixed Traffic	10
Class 3 0-6-0	Freight Tank	15
		126

V

W. A. Stanier

1932-1939

IN the 1930's steam traction attained its high noon, not only in this country but throughout the world, not only on the L.M.S., but on the three other British Railway groups. Performance and efficiency approached the highest level attainable within the Stephensonian conception. What had once been possible only by special effort on special occasions, with selected fuel, became general, despite economic and staff problems which were already beginning to bear heavily upon this form of motive power. From this time forward, until the completion of the last steam engine in 1960, no better running performances were achieved and little more power was won for each B.T.U. of calorific value in the fuel. Only mechanical improvements towards reduced maintenance cost continued to progress, some of which were left unfinished at the end of the day, before other forms of motive power took over.

In January 1932 William Stanier was appointed Chief Mechanical Engineer of the L.M.S., and this marked a turning point in the coherence and consistency of its rolling stock policy. It was late in the day for both parties, Stanier being already 55 years of age, and the L.M.S. having only 15 years of independent existence before it, five of them war years. Nevertheless, with such industry did the new broom sweep out the Augean stables, that by the last peace year of 1939, in a space of only seven years, 1,224 steam locomotives had been built to 11 new designs. Technical features were introduced into these, and also into some of the more important previous types, which raised the whole level of reliability and shopping mileage. The greater part of this design effort was concentrated within the years 1932, 1933 and 1934; only the most famous of them all, the 'Princess Coronation' was on the boards as late as 1936.

Stanier's career both before and after his advent at Euston, has been excellently protrayed[1,2] and all that his locomotives were,

[1] *Master Builders of Steam*—H. A. V. Bulleid (Ian Allan 1963).
[2] *William Stanier*—O. S. Nock (Ian Allan 1964).

and did, has been chronicled again and again. In this account I shall therefore try to avoid the well-known points and confine myself to aspects which came particularly within my purview and which carry forward the broad stream of development.

Stanier was big in stature and in mind, and we quickly realized that he was no doctrinaire. Although chosen by the powerful and imaginative team now running the railway, under Sir Josiah Stamp, for the express purpose of initiating a positive mechanical engineering policy for the L.M.S. on the lines of that so brilliantly conferred upon the G.W.R. by Churchward, he did not immediately or blindly graft Swindon practice as a whole on to his new charge. His other outstanding characteristic was that when he found he had made a mistake, and being human he was no less prone than other mortals, he would never seek to cover up bad engineering by worse, but would change direction quickly and completely, without wasting a moment of further time on what had proved unsatisfactory. In keeping with this trait he was not a man of many words. He gave his instructions in brief terms; when the resulting schemes were put before him, he was apt to accept or reject with a minimum of comment. He was the antithesis of the committee type, and was fortunate in finding himself in absolute charge of his own department, without the corroding diversification of policy and managerial direction to which his later followers have been sometimes subject. Above all he was human and kindly, and could talk to the tool fitter, the draughtsman or the engine driver in language which they understood.

With the new chief came changes in the team with whom, and through whom, the work of the C.M.E. was carried out. The small headquarters office at Euston was strengthened by the appointment of two mechanical inspectors, Read and Duncan, who were the eyes and ears of the department out in the sheds, and who took over the work previously done by Bramley and myself. From the first, I became involved in the preliminary technical scheming of the series of new locomotive designs, which were then sent to the production drawing offices of Derby, Crewe and Horwich. Before long a small drawing office was set up under my charge in an old house in Ampthill Square, in order to amplify what was passed down the line.

Symes remained as Locomotive Assistant for 18 months and thereafter was promoted to Chief Stores Superintendent. He was followed by R. A. Riddles, a Crewe man whose interest in, and

Plate 36. Stanier two-cylinder 2–6–4T No. 42540 climbs towards the summit of the Chilterns near Great Missenden, with an up London Transport Aylesbury-Baker Street train.

Plate 37. Three-cylinder parallel boiler 5X (' Patriot ') class 4–6–0 No. 45538 heads an up express near Leighton Buzzard.

Plate 38. Three-cylinder taper boiler 5X ('Jubilee') class 4–6–0 No. 45595 (originally having low superheat) accelerates through Watford with an

Plate 39. First arrival of Stanier Pacific No. 6200 *The Princess Royal* at Willesden on August 13th, 1933.

Plate 40. The first Stanier taper boiler 2–6–0 with 'coffee-pot' safety valve casing, in Crewe Works yard, in 1933.

Plate 41. Stanier 2–8–0 No. 48440 heads an empty stock train near Radlett.

Plate 42. Stanier class 5 4–6–0 No. 45278 passes Bushey with an up Northampton train.

loyalty to, that centre was mainly concentrated upon the maintenance and workshop side. His experience had been leavened by a spell at Derby, and in my later time in the drawing office there I had often seen him striding towards the shops with H. G. Ivatt to whom he was Assistant Works Superintendent. Riddles represented a new generation from the ancient Cheshire seat of tradition. He wasted no time in pining over the departed glories of 'Princes' and 'Claughtons' and entered with zest into all that Stanier was undertaking in locomotive design. Nonetheless it was the puckish streak in his make-up which many years later exacted a belated revenge for some of the indignities Crewe had suffered by causing the Midland Compounds (and other engines) to be painted and lined in L.N.W. colours.

In the same period Beames, finding himself less and less part of the new era, gracefully retired. In the design front line Gass had also retired at Horwich, being replaced by T. F. Coleman from the former North Stafford Railway. Coleman made a big impression on Stanier who transferred him to Crewe in 1933, but Coleman still retained overlordship of Horwich, now only a kind of out-station. Grover, former Chief Draughtsman at Crewe, was found other work. Chambers continued in charge at Derby with the same team as before. The new designs were apportioned between Coleman and Chambers, and although they were intended to be completely standardised, it has always been possible for the enthusiast to identify fascinating small differences in detail between a Crewe and a Derby designed product of this era.

In only one sphere was Stanier no better off than his predecessors had been, in that he had to face the retention of a separate Motive Power Department, jointly responsible to the Operating Department, in a manner which could generate so much mischief. Anderson retired before long and was replaced by D. C. Urie, son of *the* Urie of the old L.S.W.R., and formerly Mechanical Engineer in charge of the Scottish lines. He, like his predecessors, clave to the operating side of his dual responsibility and whereas Anderson used to chastise our department with whips, Urie was apt to chastise it with scorpions.

Before turning to the new designs themselves, it may be well to refer to the various features which were applied to all of them, and which made up the sum total of the Stanier "marque". By far the most important in the long run was the improvement in bearings. The shortcomings of the manganese bronze axleboxes with which engines of the Midland school were fitted were described in the last chapter. The pressed-in brass in the steel box of the Crewe school gave a firmer bearing foundation, but was associated with execrable lubrication. The Swindon axlebox was also of steel with a pressed-in brass. However, by lengthening the 'legs' of the box and increasing the distance between the centre-line of the journal and that of the pin which secured the spring link below, it had been possible to leave room for a generous sized underkeep. This could be slid out for inspection without dismantling anything else, and contained a massive oil pad of worsted and horsehair, spring loaded against the underside of the bearing. Auxiliary felt pads let into the side of this underkeep lubricated the wheel boss face. Having brought this design to the L.M.S. Stanier went further and, retaining the mechanical lubrication which he found as standard practice, he arranged for the oil therefrom to be fed into areas of minimum bearing pressure along the horizontal centre line of the box. It was then carried up the wedge-shaped working clearance between journal and brass, and delivered into the areas of maximum bearing pressure. The underkeep itself held a generous quantity of oil which could be separately topped up from the driver's long feeder, and this alone was able to sustain adequate journal lubrication for long periods should any interruption occur to the mechanical lubrication above. Lastly, by introducing new standards of accuracy and finish in the machining of the bearing surfaces themselves, it was eventually possible to do away with the crude process of scraping and fitting which was the cause of so much trouble. So effective was this introduction that in 1939, 1,224 engines so equipped had only 122 hot-coupled boxes between them, while 2,021 of the previous range of standard types had 1,140. Any one locomotive now had the probability of only one hot box in each 10 years, and this meant greatly improved availability and reduction in maintenance man hours.

Besides axleboxes, the lubrication of connecting and side rods was much improved by the interposing of felt pads the better to distribute the oil over the bearing, and perforated bronze wearing rings held lateral wear to acceptable limits.

Another innovation was to recast the whole design and practice of wheel centres, balance weights, and tyre assembly. Although the wild days of the immediate post-war period were over, when Rugby station could be 'shelled' by a disintegrating Claughton tyre as if it had been in a front line battle, none the less there had been 18 broken locomotive tyres in 1931 and 17 in 1932, and even one of these was one too many from the point of view of public safety. By fastening the tyres by the Gibson ring it was possible to avoid all drilling of the tyre itself, frequent cause of fatigue flaws, and by demanding a much higher finish of the mating parts, closer tolerances of the shrinkage allowance could be achieved. To limit flexing of the tyre material between spokes a stiff triangular rim was provided on all wheel centres; and for the sake of uniformity of support all round the tyre the previous cast-in balance weights were replaced by separate plates riveted together, between which lead weights provided the appropriate balance. These measures, in conjunction with developments with the steel makers in the direction of greater ductility without sacrifice of hardness, finally exorcised tyre breakage as a feature of the locomotive scene other than the most exceptional circumstances.

To cylinders, valves and valve gears as already existing in their most recent form Stanier brought few changes. He recognised that this aspect of L.M.S. design had already assured excellent results, and in particular he made no attempt to replace the six ring valve head by the Swindon semi-plug type. He did, however, introduce the screwed-on Western piston and also the 'rope' piston rod packing of his former company, but these were two features, which along with a few others, were never successful when transplanted and both were superseded in the fullness of time.

The introduction of the taper boiler has always been considered Stanier's sign manual, and he himself indicated that this was one of his most important contributions. Certainly the Swindon version had through the years been brought to a high level of perfection in construction, stay fitting and so on, and L.M. boiler practice benefited greatly from application of these ideas. The taper form as such, however, while giving some small advantage in output to weight ratio, was only really essential in the larger sizes, and for medium and small boilers was a debatable matter. Stanier firmly believed that the arrangement of water and steam spaces gave, in combination, advantage in steam production. He explained to us that these elements would counterbalance the effects of the low degree superheat which was a feature of Swindon practice, and which he now applied to all of his first designs for the L.M.S. This, however, turned out not to be the case, and with some 100°F. lower steam temperatures his earlier engines were at a disadvantage. All credit to him, therefore, that as soon as he was assured of this, he set about providing 3 and 4 row superheaters to both existing and further new locomotives which restored their thermal performance to the highest levels. It was more than 10 years later that the same realisation came to Swindon itself. At first a wholesale fitting of taper boilers was visualised on existing as well as on new types, and an early scheme portrayed six sets of flanging blocks, which in 12 combinations of tube and firebox lengths defined boilers which could be used on no less than 4,235 existing or rebuilt L.M.S. engines, including even the Midland Compounds, and Derby and Crewe 0–8–0's. In the outcome, however, except for oddments, nothing was rebuilt with taper boilers in Stanier's time.

Of other more detailed introductions some went well and some did not. For example, earlier boilers were domeless, a steam collector pipe leading to a regulator combined with the superheater header in the smokebox. This arrangement not only demanded separate means of lubrication, but with the mixtures of waters encountered on the L.M.S., including a proportion of softened water, priming occurred against which the low level of the steam intake did not offer much protection. Domes with sliding regulators set horizontally at the highest practicable point within the loading gauge soon joined the larger superheaters as a 'must' for all further construction. Top feed clacks at first followed Swindon design exactly, but were soon in trouble and a number of versions were subsequently developed, none of which prevented the occasional rusty line round the boiler where copious leakage of feed water deployed itself inside the clothing. The Derby injector was retained and it was not until nationalisation, long after Stanier, that the Swindon injector, much superior, was adopted. Two very good features were the Western smokebox and bogie. The smokebox itself gave ample volume and good air tightness, and the Swindon formula for blastpipe and chimney proportions promoted excellent front end conditions, at least for engines having 4 beats per revolution. On the other hand internal deflector plates, supposed to equalise the draught over the tubes and reduce spark emission, not having the decisive virtues of the full American self-cleaning front end, proved a great pest to motive power staff. In due course large piles of this ironmongery began to be accumulated in out of the way spots behind shed premises. The bogie carried the engine front end on two pads set well out under the frames, and the side control springs, in parallel before and behind the centre casting, gave positive control throughout the range of movement in a manner the Fowler bogie was unable to do.

In coming to a 'Three-cylinder' railway Stanier hesitated at first, wondering if he should not himself opt for this principle.

The work of the 'Royal Scots' and of the two 'Rebuilt Claughtons' commanded respect. When I was set to work in March on diagrams for his initial consideration, schemes were worked out for four 3-cylinder types, a Pacific, a Mixed Traffic 4–6–0 to supersede the 'Prince of Wales', a 2–8–0 to replace the Fowler 0–8–0, and a 2–6–4 Tank to meet urgent power requirements on the Tilbury line. However, only the latter retained its three cylinders through to actual construction, the Chief no doubt being influenced by some of Gresley's claims from the other side of the country, including that of quicker acceleration. 37 of these engines, so much better than the indigenous 4–4–2 Tanks, found much acceptance, and operated the arduous Southend traffic for many years with the sweet running of well-oiled sewing machines. On the other hand, when tried on the Northern Suburban lines, where the Fowler 2–6–4 Tanks were well entrenched, they showed no superiority whatever, neither in acceleration, steaming, coal consumption, nor anything else claimed on behalf of 3-cylinders. Stanier at once grasped the realities of the situation and had a 2-cylinder version quickly drawn out at Derby. The first of these latter appeared a year later in 1935, forerunner of 206 similar engines which spread all over the system before further changes were made in Fairburn's time (Plate 36). Another 3-cylinder locomotive of the Stanier series was the so-called 5X class, now leader of the 'second eleven' of express passenger engines. Mention was made in the last chapter of the decision to gradually replace the 'Claughtons' by the Derby designed 3-cylinder version, and by the beginning of 1932 much material had been ordered for a further series. The new engines were badly needed, and Stanier agreed to their construction but delayed their completion in order to introduce for the first time some of his specialities referred to above; of which improved axleboxes, wheels, bogies and tyres were the principal. The general design, including the enlarged Claughton boiler, remained unaltered (Plate 37).

Besides the original two, 50 more were turned out under the new regime in 1932/3/4, all of which carried the above-mentioned features except the first ten, Nos. 5502–5511, which retained the radial bogie from the 'Claughton'.

This group of parallel boiler 5X class engines turned out to be something of a rod for Stanier's back, and it was the instrument by which his mind was quickly turned away from low degree superheat.

Leaving the chassis part unaltered except for 17″ instead of 18″ dia. cylinders, a taper boiler was designed to supersede the enlarged Claughton boiler within the same weight, having 225 lbs. working pressure, but only a 14-element superheater in place of a 24-element apparatus. The new boiler contained every feature of good circulation and improved manufacture which Stanier believed in.

The first such engine was turned out in 1934, part of a series of 90 produced within the 12 months (Plate 38). They were immediately allocated to the exacting Euston to Birmingham expresses but to everybody's consternation showed themselves barely equal to the former engines in efficiency on test, and definitely inferior in steam-producing capacity in daily service. There turned out to be several reasons for this. The reduction of nearly 100°F. in steam temperature was a pure loss to thermal efficiency, which no other feature in the design did in fact do anything to counterbalance. Secondly, the contraction in the diameter of the front tubeplate due to the taper shape, plus the theory that the circulation arising from widely spaced tubes would help steaming, both resulted in a reduction in the total tube-free area through which the hot gases pass from the firebox to the smokebox. This value is very critical to a boiler's performance, an area of 15% of the grate area representing free steaming, the area of 13% which this boiler had, imposed a severe upper limit to the ability to boil water. Thirdly, the blast pipe and chimney dimensions were based upon the Swindon formula, which was designed for 4-beat engines, and was no use at all for 6-beat engines at large outputs, as the resultant draught was insufficient. A situation arose, therefore, which was very serious for a while, and there was considerable recrimination from the motive power and operating sides.

It was characteristic of Stanier that he set his people to work with great energy to rectify matters, but in the absence of a stationary test plant it took a good deal of trial and error work, over many anxious months, before the steaming was put right. Things got worse before they got better. In the first phase of modification, although the superheater was stepped up to 21 elements and the tube bank augmented to give the required 15% of total free area in relation to grate, the further mistake was made of altering the relationship of area to surface in the individual tubes. Consequently the hot gases passed at excessive velocity through the boiler, reaching the smokebox at too high a temperature, with resulting loss in efficiency.

A third and last modification was made with a larger number of small tubes of less diameter with some adjustment to the proportions of the superheater, which now had 24 elements, and this, with a final reduction of blast pipe diameter from $5\frac{1}{4}''$ to $4\frac{7}{8}''$ diameter, at last produced a combination which permitted these engines to take their place as honoured members of the Stanier locomotive heirachy. They surpassed, in their turn, the parallel boiler engines which were renowned in their heyday. To those interested in technical details this tuning-up process has been described in a published paper,[1] and the lessons learned were soon applied as regards superheater and tube proportions, to most of the other types in the new series now to be described.

It can be deduced that one of Stanier's remits, from his new management, was to provide a locomotive which would surpass the performance of the 'Royal Scot' by running through to Glasgow, whereas the latter was limited to the 300-mile stretch from Euston to Carlisle. The larger firebox and ashpan capacity, necessary for this requirement, could only be satisfied by a 'Pacific'. This project was pursued with great gusto since that the East Coast route had had a 10-year start in the introduction of this kind of machine. The engine was first schemed in both 3- and 4-cylinder form, both having 6′ 9″ diameter coupled wheels. The former (Fig. 18) was a very straightforward layout which would have used the Royal Scot cylinder centres and valve gear. Deciding finally upon the latter, the next stage was to explore different tube and combustion chamber lengths. By the end of April the final diagram was ready for Derby, with wheel diameter reduced to 6′ 6″, arriving at a front end similar in its disposition to that of the 'King' class, except for the use of four independent valve gears. For his first six months or so Stanier accepted the idea of the stovepipe chimney, left over from the previous regime, and this emblem adorned all our initial schemes. As the 'Pacific' project approached finality, however, he began to flinch. The diagram which eventually went to Derby for production carried a version of MacIntosh's Caledonian chimney, out of which Chambers and his men eventually fashioned the attractive shape which adorned this and all further Stanier engines. It was also at this time that use of the Caledonian siren was decided upon. Students may have been puzzled by a published photograph of the second engine of this class No. 6201, having a double stovepipe chimney.

[1] "Locomotive Boiler Design—Theory and Practice"—Loubser and Cox (*Journal* I.L.E. No. 144, 1938).

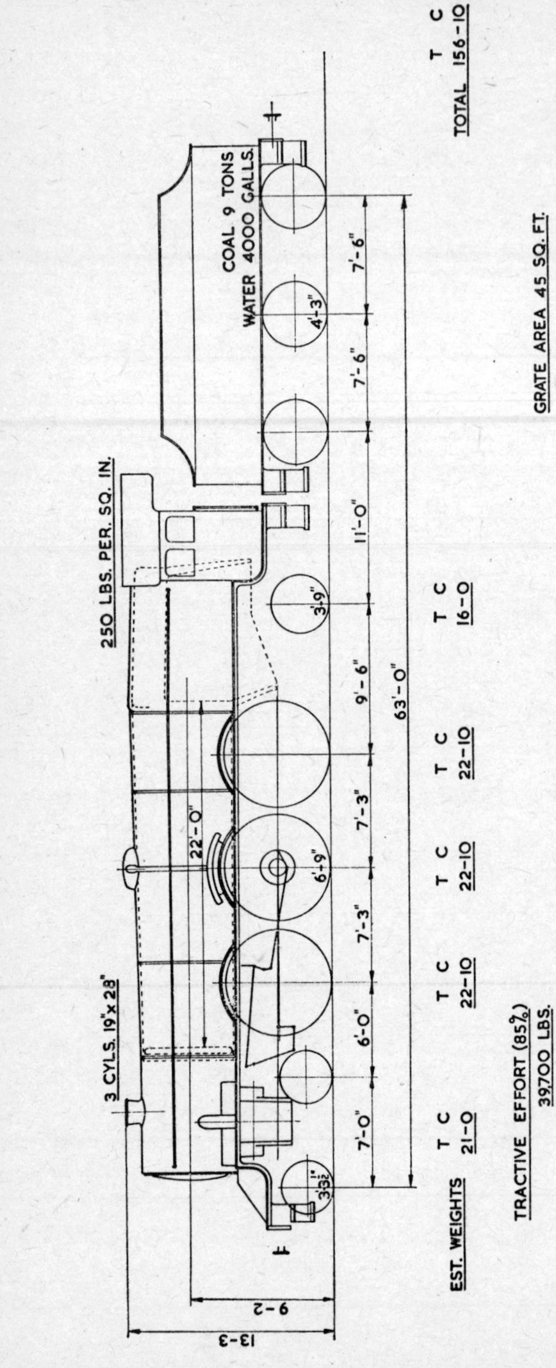

PROPOSED 3-CYLINDER 4-6-2 PASSENGER ENGINE.

Fig. 18

This was, however, only fitted as a later experiment, in which the exhausts from the inside and outside cylinders were separately evacuated, without first mingling together in a common chamber, as is usually the case with double exhausts. This arrangement was highly unsuccessful and was quickly removed.

In August 1933 No. 6200, *The Princess Royal*, came down from Crewe to Willesden one Sunday and successfully passed its clearance tests in Euston station (Plate 39). Soon after, it made its first demonstration run with Dynamometer Car, and so passed with its eventual 11 sisters into a creditable future which has been well documented.

I had very little directly to do with the 'Turbomotive', No. 6202, last of the three initial 'Pacific' prototypes turned out in 1935. R. C. Bond[1] has already given a most detailed account of its inception, design and performance, and the only point to be made here is that once more a modest and most promising departure from the classic steam locomotive form, was not able to provide any real justification for its continuance.

The first Stanier engine actually to take the rails in 1933 was none of the foregoing, but 2–6–0 No. 13245, one of a series of 40 to meet the continuing demand for mixed traffic engines of this kind. Whereas the multi-cylinder types already referred to presented no problems as regards the loading gauge, a serious initial difficulty had to be overcome at once before the series of 2-cylinder types, backbone of the projected standard range, could be proceeded with. It was desired to avoid the extreme and rather clumsy inclination of the outside cylinders, such as had had to be used on the Horwich 2–6–0's. Although the adoption of 225 lbs. per sq. in. boiler pressure permitted cylinder diameter to be reduced from 21″ to 18½″, the Civil Engineers' reply to the first 2–6–0 diagram with horizontal cylinders was 21 pages of running restrictions, all due to the width over cylinders being considered so great as to foul the platforms. Rather than knuckle under to this as his predecessors had been obliged to do, Stanier forced the issue and demanded proof. Accordingly three of the Horwich engines were fitted up with lead fingers arranged at platform level in simulation of the profile of the proposed new horizontal cylinders. These engines in quick succession visited 314 places in England and Wales, platforms, crossovers and loading bays, where the clearance was thought to be tight, and any 'foul' could immediately be discovered by the

[1] "Ten Years' Experience with the L.M.S. Non-condensing Turbine Locomotive No. 6206"—R. C. Bond (*Journal* I.L.E. No. 191, 1946).

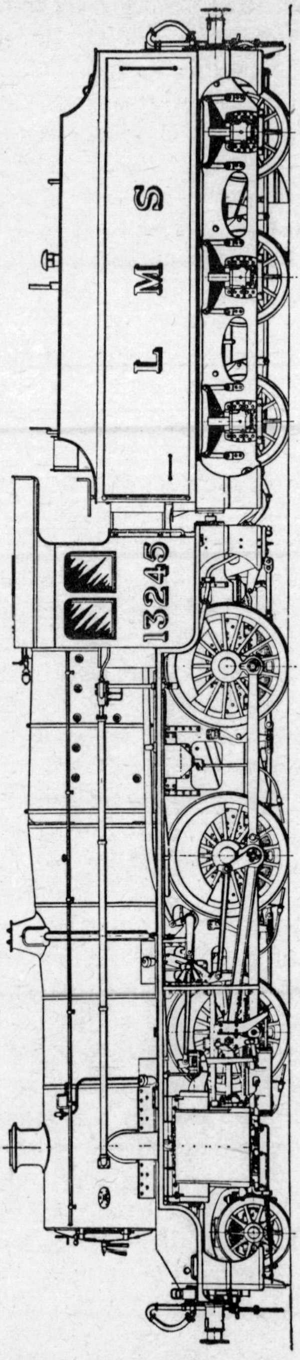

Fig. 19. First Stanier taper boiler 2–6–0 with 'coffee-pot' safety valve casing. Built Crewe Works, 1933.

deforming of the lead strips. At only 89 of these places was clearance found to be less than 2″, and at a number of these, in turn, engines of this size were already prohibited for axle weight. So, with a negligible amount of setting back of platform coping stones at a few stations, the railway was made safe for the universal use of outside cylinders, and this bugbear of the old North Western and Midland systems was finally laid to rest.

A curious circumstance surrounds No. 13245, in that it is the only L.M.S. engine actually built with the G.W.R. 'Coffee Pot' safety valve casing. Clear minded as Stanier was upon the design features which he wished to introduce, and able as he was in producing rough sketches of details, he never to my knowledge actually sketched out a whole locomotive as he would like it. Accordingly in making diagrams for him to discuss, we had to imagine his mind on a number of matters. The very first such diagram made in the March after he took over, depicted the 3-cylinder 4–6–0 and 2–8–0 combination he wished to see schemed out, and as Fig. 20 shows we tentatively indicated thereon a Swindon 'coffee pot'. He quickly made it clear that he did not want his engines to look like carbon copies of Western practice, and we then worked out a dome-like cover to the top-feed clacks on the otherwise domeless boilers. As Fig. 21 indicates all further diagrams embodied this feature, which was applied to the first standard range, before real domes and high degree superheat were introduced.

Certainly the official diagram for the 2–6–0 sent out from Euston in April had this small dome cover over the top feeds. Nevertheless, owing to some misunderstanding, the 'coffee pot' became reincorporated into the production drawings. When the engine emerged from Crewe erecting shop it was not well received by the chief, who promptly caused the offending member to be removed, and what he had ordained was substituted. All official photographs were destroyed, but the indefatigable late W. H. Whitworth is believed to have secured the snap which is represented in Plate 40. This is one of the little by-ways of locomotive history, not of the slightest importance in itself, which intrigues the student, and lightens his journey through more serious affairs.

The centre piece of the new standard series was the 2-cylinder 4–6–0/2–8–0 group which by the end of the L.M.S. accounted for 60% of the total 'Stanier' output. As at first outlined with 3-cylinders (Fig. 20) the intention was once again to use substantially the 'Royal Scot' cylinders and valve gear, the former suitably reduced in diameter, and this diagram was the only other place,

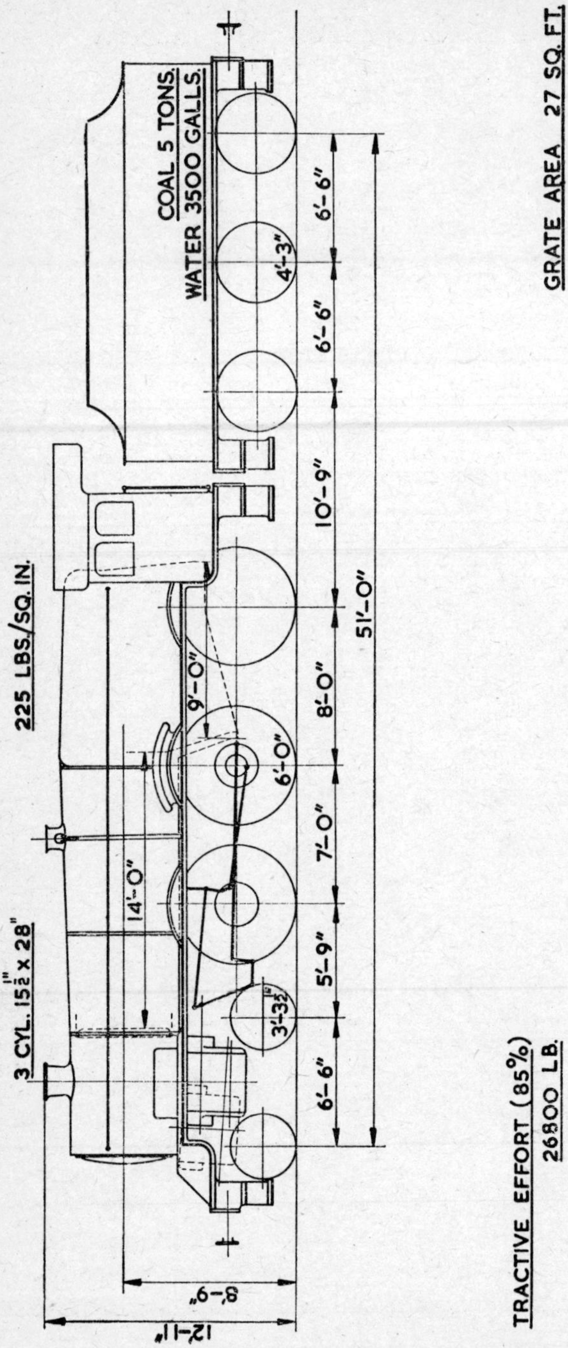

PROPOSED 3 CYL. CLASS 5.

Fig. 20

other than on the 2–6–0 already mentioned, where the unauthorised coffee pot ever appeared. From the experience with the 2–6–4 Tank no effect whatever was likely to have resulted from using 3 cylinders, other than increase in weight and cost. To say that these engines as built filled a long-felt want is an understatement. The versatility of the 4–6–0 Mixed Traffic type exceeded all expectations, while the 2–8–0, although employed on less spectacular services, took over the central burden of freight haulage all over the system. In the war years it even put in a good stint of regular passenger working between Glasgow and Aberdeen (Plate 41). Although disguised with stovepipe chimneys, dome-shaped top feed covers and side window cabs, the diagrams which finally left Euston owed a good deal in their conception to G.W.R. Hall and 2800 classes (Fig 21). At Crewe Coleman, to whom the production design was entrusted, at once imposed his own individuality upon these projects and reassembled them in a manner which produced much more balanced designs, adjusting the boiler heights and bringing the centre of gravity forward. These two designs were notable in another facet in that they both went straight into traffic in 1934 and 1935 respectively in quantity, without teething troubles or initial modifications. The Mixed Traffic engine in particular was so good in basic conception, that it proved worthy of steady development over the next 15 years (Plate 42).

The smallest of the new range was also the least satisfactory, namely the Class 3 2–6–2 Tank (Plate 43). Instead of breaking away completely, Stanier merely revamped the already unsatisfactory Derby engine, retaining the same spread-out wheelbase, tractive effort and grate area. Certainly the whole engine was redesigned with taper boiler, new cylinders, cab tanks and bunker, and with long travel valve gear, but it was still under-boilered. Many changes were made subsequently, such as increasing the grate area from 17.5 to 19.2 sq. ft., introducing a modernised version of the Adams 'Vortex' blast pipe, and most drastic move of all, the rebuilding of three engines with larger diameter boilers. Nothing sufficed, however, to make this class better than very pedestrian, and I recall how unsatisfactory they were on the St. Pancras suburban services before they were entirely replaced by 2–6–4 Tanks soon after nationalisation.

There was only one locomotive in this first phase which was seriously discussed, but which did not reach fruition, namely a Class 4 4–6–0 for Scotland. The boilers were running out on a mixed group of 21 Callander and Oban and ex-Highland Jones Goods

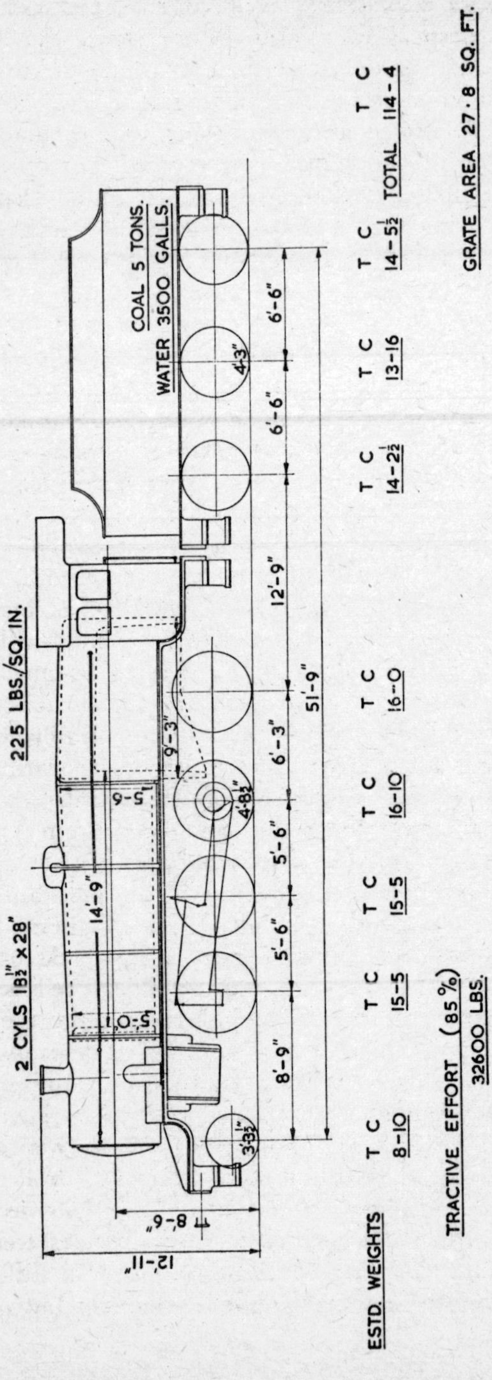

PROPOSED 2 CYLINDER 2-8-0 FREIGHT ENGINE.

Fig. 21

4–6–0's, and it seemed senseless to reboiler such outmoded classes. On the other hand an axle load limitation of some 15½ tons ruled out every modern standard type. Accordingly a scheme was prepared for the light ten-wheeler shown in Fig. 22 which was a scaled-down version of the Class 5, having a maximum estimated axle load of 15 tons 15 cwt. Contemplation of such a proposal raised no enthusiasm in the breasts of the Motive Power Department, and Urie, who knew Scotland well, quickly appreciated that it offered no improvement in pulling power, even if it was more efficient and could run faster when it had a chance. Ten of these engines actually found their way on to the 1934 building programme with the intention of following on with 11 more in 1935. However, here again a powerful *demarche* was made against the Civil Engineers, with the result that some bridge rebuilding was undertaken, which permitted first of all Highland 'Clan' class locomotives, and later on the Stanier 'Black Fives' themselves to run to Oban, solving the problem in a more satisfactory manner.

This concludes the new design effort up to the end of 1934, and apart from the 5X class engines referred to above, the only other existing type which was altered was the 'Royal Scot' class. It had been decided to send a locomotive on a good-will mission to the U.S.A., but the date which was fixed, early summer of 1933, was too soon for a new 'Pacific' to be sent. The Royal Scot which was selected had its running gear completely rebuilt with new steel axleboxes, additional frame cross stays, side bearing bogie, new wheel centres and tyres, and new silico-manganese bearing springs. The remainder of the class were soon equipped with the first two of these features with an immediate and drastic reduction in the number of hot boxes.

Among miscellaneous events with which I was concerned was an epidemic of derailments of engines having pony trucks on 1 in 8 crossovers on sharp curves. In such circumstances there is a distance of some 3″–4″ between the noses of the crossing where the leading wheels, under the centreing force of their side control arrangements, are unguided by the flanges and when lateral movement is easy, and the wheels take the wrong road. Swing link trucks, having little friction in their moving parts as on the Fowler engines were especially prone. On the Stanier engines, with spring controlled trucks having side bearing pads, either the lateral movement was equally free if lubricated, or alternatively if the side bearers were lined with dry friction material, the whole wheelbase was stiffened up and derailment occurred not now at the crossovers but on plain

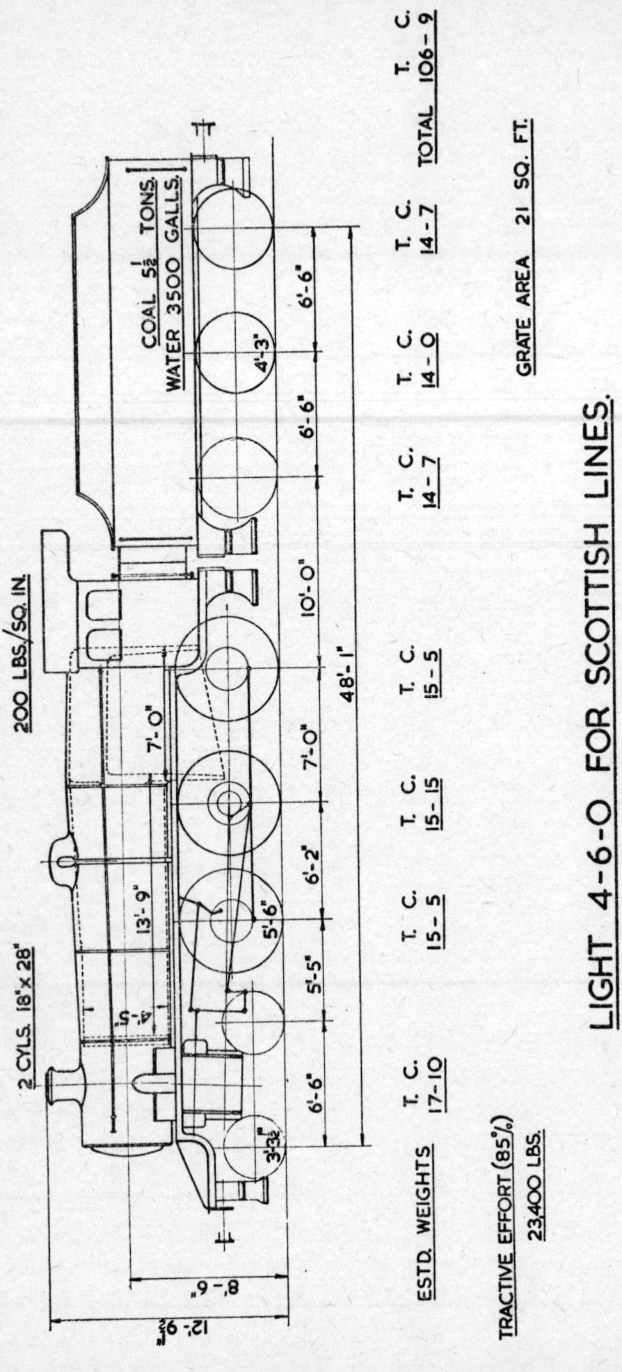
2 CYLS. 18" x 28"
200 LBS./SQ. IN.
COAL 5½ TONS.
WATER 3500 GALLS.
13'-9"
7'-0"
4'-1⅝"
12'-9⅝"
8'-6"
3'-3½"
5'-6"
4'-3"
6'-6"
5'-5"
6'-2"
7'-0"
10'-0"
6'-6"
6'-6"
48'-1"
ESTD. WEIGHTS
T. C. 17-10
T. C. 15-5
T. C. 15-15
T. C. 15-5
T. C. 14-7
T. C. 14-0
T. C. 14-7
TOTAL T. C. 106-9
TRACTIVE EFFORT (85%)
23,400 LBS.
GRATE AREA 21 SQ. FT.
LIGHT 4-6-0 FOR SCOTTISH LINES.

Fig. 22

curved track. This was a really serious problem for some time and was finally overcome by selection of a material having a controlled co-efficient of friction for the side bearers, and in the case of the swing link trucks by the addition of separate spring-loaded friction pads, slowing down the free lateral movement of the bolster sufficiently. Another interesting exercise was the re-numbering of the whole of the modern L.M.S. locomotive stock to come within 10,000. In this we fell into the usual snag of allowing insufficient space, and 500 numbers allocated to the Class 5 engines (5000–5499), which seemed so ample at the time, proved insufficient, and they had also to be given numbers backwards from 4999. We did try at this time to get acceptance for the mid-European idea of having a type number for each class, with a thousamd vacant numbers to follow, all within 5 figures—but this was ruled out as too un-English!

Early in 1934 I undertook something which contributed to turning my career aside for a time into an unexpected direction. Since the move to Euston an officers' conference had been initiated as an annual event, in which senior and middle officers gave papers or contributed to discussion in the presence of top management. In this year I was pressed into 'volunteering' a paper on "Built-up Crank Axles". This being the very first time I had ventured upon such an undertaking in public, my knees shook and my heart palpitated much more than perhaps showed outwardly. In this paper I dwelt only a little upon design, but went to town on manufacture, repair, and costs. While I do not suppose this was the only cause, it was, I am sure, one of the causes due for my being called into Stanier's presence at the end of the same year. I was commanded to start forthwith at Derby Locomotive Works as Assistant Works Superintendent; straight from 'draughtsman' to second man in a works of 4,000 men, where I spent the next two years.

I have never in my railway career come across a more curious appointment. It was over 13 years since I had worked inside the shops, and then only as an apprentice. It is true that in all my technical and design work I had a strong instinct as to how it should be made and repaired, and that I had paid many visits to works in consequence. But that was not the same thing as experience in progress and production planning, machine loading, piecework prices, labour relations, and organisation of repair work, all of which I now started to learn the hard way—that is from scratch. It is not easy to imagine what reaction my superiors expected from this drastic throwing of the baby into the pond. Many men have passed from the drawing office back into the workshops and have made good, but usually via the lower ranks of assistants where they could learn the ropes in relative obscurity. I had an unusual entry on two counts. Firstly, because I was started practically at the top, and secondly because, as will presently be told, the job under my predecessor had dwindled almost to a vacuum. If they wanted a young man, I was a very young 34, if they wanted a fresh mind, mine was so fresh on the subject of works management as to be almost vacuous, if they wanted somebody cheap, my appointment at a salary of £500 did not strain the company's finances. The temptation to dramatise early hardships must be resisted, however, when it is recalled that in my newly married state five hundred a year then provided a car and a housemaid, and that the job provided a private office and a personal clerk, status symbols which I found it very agreeable to encounter for the first time.

Strangely enough my two years in the works turned out to be a happy, and to me useful period, and although it formed an interlude in my lifelong connection with design development, it may be of interest to refer to some of the highlights. On Monday morning, November 12th, 1934, I walked once more across the lattice bridge from Derby Station, and turned right instead of left under the clock tower to be received by the Works Superintendent, George Bellamy. Bellamy was no stranger for I had met him a number of times in Dynamometer Car Testing days, when he was in the Motive Power department. On that day and thereafter he was a kind and considerate chief, who bore with my ignorance and put me at ease so that I could the better grapple with my strange surroundings. As assistant before me, he had had J. V. Denning, an ex-Crewe man, who was one of those occasional misfits who rise to great heights in wartime but who never become fully reconciled to civil life. He had fallen more and more behind the stream of current endeavour, with the result that the only activities I inherited directly from him were works transport and supervision of apprentices! All the work he should have been doing as deputy had been divided between F. G. Chambers and Edgar Larkin, the first of whom was brother to the Herbert Chambers in charge of the Drawing Office, and the latter of whom we last saw on the board adjacent to mine in Sanford's experimental section in the old drawing office. Larkin was another refugee from the drawing board but he had the good fortune to enter the works lower down, and was now in charge of Progress and Planning. Chambers, a tiny man with the heart of a lion, had come up the hard way from the shop floor, and by his application and ability could have aspired to the post I now occupied. He never bore any visible ill will however and like his chief went out of his way to help the newcomer. With this very pleasant trio of top management, and drawing upon a certain measure of adaptability which has fortunately been part of my make-up, I now proceeded to feel my way with the other assistants, with the foremen, and with the men. True to my earlier experiences I found the Derby atmosphere as congenial in the works as I had done in the drawing office.

The works were geared at this time to build 82 new locomotives per annum, and to repairing an allocation 2,500 engines, almost entirely former Midland and Fowler standard types, which involved a weekly output of 20 repairs. While not such a showpiece as Crewe, it nevertheless followed the same principles, although carrying them out in a different way. In the last few weeks of 1934, after I arrived, there was an intense effort going on to complete a batch of 10 taper boiler 5X class 4–6–0's which for some actuarial reason it was thought a matter of life and death to have completed by December 31st. Overtime was freely resorted to, and Bellamy ranged the shops giving pep talks to the men from the top of benches or nearby castings. All this effort met with a bleak response, however, when in the next year the price was totted up, and the cost per engine turned out to be well above the norm. It was then discovered to be a little vague as to who had ordered the crash exercise in the first place. Most of 1935 was occupied in building a group of 74 Stanier 2–6–2 Tanks, and at the end of that year and thereafter during my time, Derby reverted to 2–6–4 Tanks which were its real speciality.

The main repair effort was in Chambers' hands, and if I did not contribute much, I at least learned a great deal which has stood me in good stead in later activities. Naturally all kinds of special jobs came my way among which were investigations into works transport, valve setting methods, outdoor machinery organisation, use of compressed air, analysis of repair costs and I kept an eye on the two 'outstation' shops at Bristol and Sheffield. I was also involved in the outcome of two bad derailments with Deeley 0–6–4 Tanks Nos. 2011 and 2013. In these cases the presence of a 'Cartazzi' assembly at the leading coupled axlebox position, plus a trailing bogie having an ineffectual centering action combined to set up side sway and eventual wheel lifting when indifferent track was transversed. No. 2000 was rebuilt with normal type leading boxes and improved bogie, but as the class as a whole was something of an assembly of lame ducks, it was soon decided to scrap the lot.

It was in this connection I met the Chief Inspecting Officer of Railways, then Colonel but one day to become Sir Alan Mount. Nothing told me that I was, in the not very distant future, to tour India in his company, and to work hard with him during a war which only now began to appear as a grim and distant possibility.

I began at this time to be active in the affairs of the Institution of Locomotive Engineers, which held its Midland centre meetings in Birmingham. I was at once put on the committee, and again commanded to volunteer a paper, my first effort for the Institution being rather naturally an expansion of what I gave before the Officers' Conference in 1934, entitled this time "Locomotive Wheels, Tyres and Axles".

Now fate again intervened, and I was as abruptly removed from the workshops as I had been hi-jacked into them. It must have been clear to authority that whatever I might be learning of value to myself, I was not of the stuff of which great works managers were made, although I have little doubt that in the long run I could have done at least as well as some who have followed me in that capacity. Thus, in November 1936, almost two years to the day after I received my first orders, I was again summoned into Stanier's presence and in a minimum of words, and without commentary on my past performance, was commanded to transfer forthwith to the Derby Drawing Office where as Development Assistant I was to set up a new section for forward thinking on design matters. I naturally took this a little hard, and the change from helping to control 4,000 men to being in charge of only four, seemed at first a rather drastic demotion. Nevertheless with over 25 years of hindsight with which I now review the event, I can only say thank goodness the change was made, for my true flair and happiness has always lain with Design.

I now passed under the control of T. F. Coleman, who upon translation of Herbert Chambers to Euston as Locomotive Assistant had been put in charge of all production design with headquarters at Derby. A huge man of gargoyle-like features, his blunt and craggy manner made short work of the remaining independence of Derby, Crewe and Horwich, and thenceforth design knew its master, who wielded undisputed sway in the former temples of disharmony. In the main office the last drawings were being turned out for Stanier's masterpiece, the Coronation Scot class of which the first five were completed in streamlined form in the same year. This was, in effect, a redesign of the Princess Royal engine in which Coleman was given *carte blanche* to increase the boiler capacity and rearrange the general proportions into a much more harmonious relationship. The 6′ 9″ diameter wheels, originally postulated in the earliest schemes of 1932, were restored, and all vestiges of the Western 'King' class were swept away in a cylinder and valve gear layout which, under Coleman's influence, undoubtedly stemmed from that of the Hughes rebuilt 4–6–0's. In this engine was finally combined, in its most effective form, those Swindon importations which had proved of most value, together with L.M.S. survivals to which new thinking on Boiler and Superheat proportions, plus enlargement of streamlined ports and passages made a noteworthy contribution.

The work undertaken in the new development section in the year in which I was in charge of it was of some interest. On the locomotive side, schemes were prepared for a High Pressure Turbine Electric locomotive, a 2-cylinder version of the 5X class 4–6–0 engine, and some moves towards designing something to take the place of the obsolescent Fowler type 4 0–6–0 engine which reigned supreme in the middle range of Freight Motive Power.

The exercise on the Turbine-Electric engine was suggested by the availability at that time of three new types of high pressure boiler recently developed for locomotive purposes. These were the Velox, a drum-type water-tube boiler having forced circulation and combustion under pressure, the 'Steamotive', a once through 'flash' type boiler, with automatically controlled oil firing, something on the lines of the 'Vapor' boiler with which we are now so familiar on diesels, and finally the Lamont, also a water-tube and drum-type boiler having forced circulation, but capable of burning coal under manual operation. Notwithstanding the unhappy experience with the Schmidt-Henschel boiler already referred to, high pressure did seem in these pre-diesel days one method of raising the low thermal efficiency of steam traction. I made my first visit abroad in February 1937 in company with Herbert Chambers, to examine the Velox boiler in Paris, where a prototype was being mounted on the chassis of an old P.L.M. compound 4–6–0. Although this effort was eventually put to work, and I rode on it on a subsequent visit in 1938, it was really a most complex piece of machinery which did not commend itself to British operating conditions. The boiler selected for our own scheme was the Lamont, which alone of the alternatives could be served with coal in the ordinary way. The locomotive as worked out followed the principle of the Beyer Peacock-Ljungström engine in that the boiler, fuel and water ran on one unit, the turbo-generator and air-cooled condenser on the other, a major difference was that both units were mounted on conventional motor bogies. Each unit was 52′ long and diesel-type cabs were provided at the outer ends. The fireman was to occupy a compartment amidships in the boiler unit, and he might have found the climate rather warm, as did the unfortunate fireman who took out Bulleids 'Leader' engine having a similarly placed 'glory hole' some ten years later. Total weight was about 184 tons, and 3,000 h.p. at the traction motors was proposed, which would have given a sustained performance substantially above that of the existing Pacifics. When full advantage was taken of the theoretical improvement in efficiency, the coal price of £1 per ton ruling at the time only offered a 10% return on an increased capital cost of some £3,000, and such a machine was bound to cost far more than that beyond conventional practice. For this reason the proposal was dropped, and recalling subsequent experiences in this field in different parts of the world, few regrets remain.

With two cylinders 19¼″ × 28″, in conjunction with 250 lbs. boiler pressure, the possible filleting of the inside cylinders of the 5X class was prompted; firstly as a means of getting more boiler capacity on to the same weight of engine, and secondly by a good deal of trouble with inside big ends current at the time. The weight saved would permit a shortened version of the large taper boiler already designed for Royal Scot No. 6170 to be fitted. However, gradual easement of civil engineering restrictions in due course permitted this boiler to be fitted to the unaltered 3-cylinder arrangement.

The development of a successor to the Class 4 0–6–0 Freight is a long story, and it was in fact 10 years later that the first Class 4 2–6–0 was produced. The tortuous nature of this period of gestation will be described in the next chapter, but the first blow was struck in this year by the self-obvious means of offering the 2-cylinder 2–6–4 Tank in the form of a tender engine. This was not, however, acceptable to the operating people because of route availability, and regardless of their many drawbacks, Fowler 0–6–0's continued to be built in small batches right into 1941.

The most effective action of the new section in its initial period was not, however, a locomotive design at all, but a powerful contribution to locomotive testing in the form of three mobile testing units. These, with a new Amsler Dynamometer Car, were to provide for constant speed testing of locomotives on the German model, which would permit exploration of basic design data, unobtainable with the variable speed testing in ordinary service hitherto in use. Each of the units was a kind of electric motor-coach in reverse, the motors acting as generators, and a known drawbar resistance could be imposed upon the engine to be tested by a speed sensitive control of the amount of electric power generated which was dissipated in air-cooled resistances. The whole thing could be worked from the Dynamometer Car by an elegant form of control developed by Ivan Andrews, late of English Electric Co., who was now teamed with us in the production of this novel apparatus, which turned out to be excellently suited to its purpose, and is still in active use today.

Besides the means of testing, Andrews also brought to us theories on steam locomotive testing. Nurtured, as he had been, in the ways of Professor Nordmann of the Reichsbahn he propounded methods which found no acceptance under British conditions. Long and fierce were the arguments until the approaching war required all such endeavours to be laid on one side.

In September 1937 Herbert Chambers died suddenly to the great sorrow of everyone who had known him, because of his warm personality. To fill the vacancy, thus created, I was appointed as Personal and Technical Assistant to the C.M.E. in October of that year, and as such I returned to Euston. There I found an unexpected exchange of positions had taken place. In July 1937 Riddles had been appointed Mechanical and Electrical Engineer for Scotland, and George Ivatt, who had formerly been in charge up there, was brought down to be Principal Assistant to Stanier in his stead. As mentioned earlier in this chapter Riddles had been Ivatt's assistant when the latter was in charge of Derby Works for several years from 1928 onwards, and together they had been able greatly to reduce the days in shops for locomotives under repair. They had thus both learned to sing out of the same hymn book as it were, and I did not have any great task in accommodating myself to the ways and outlook of the new incumbent.

In the interim, moreover, the department had moved from the rather unlikeable accommodation, under the eaves in the central part of the station, to a block of more modern offices on Drummond

Street to the west side of the famous Arch. Before long I shared my very pleasent office with Roland Bond who had been translated from Assistant Works Manager at Crewe to Superintending Engineer of the new Rugby Locomotive Testing Station which it had now been decided to build as a joint venture with the London North Eastern Railway. Sir Nigel Gresley had for many years campaigned for this station. A previous proposal intended to serve British Railways plus the Private Manufacturers had fallen by the wayside, since the latter were still reeling from the effects of the Depression, and had second thoughts about the expenditure. It was decided that the L.M.S. and L.N.E. were to go it alone. Bond, jointly responsible to Stanier and Gresley, concentrated upon the design, specification, and placing of orders for the different elements of the new plant.

Only one new locomotive project was worked upon in this period before approaching war put an end to such activities for some time. This was a rather important design, however, involving a 4–6–4 engine, greatly surpassing in power even the latest 4–6–2. A first published reference to it was made in my Presidential Address to the Institution of Locomotive Engineers in 1957 (Fig 23). I think it is worth enlarging upon the thinking which inspired this project, since had peace continued there was an even chance that the locomotive might have been developed and built.

The *Coronation Scot* was running to Glasgow in 6½ hours with some 300 tons trailing load. Internal air services already appearing as future competition caused serious consideration to be given to accelerating all the day trains. This meant lifting up to 500 tons in the same time, or even in 6 hours. To do this no greater starting tractive effort was needed than with the existing Pacifics, which were already handling the same load but at lower speeds. A big increase in power at the higher speeds was needed. As adhesion was not in question 6 coupled wheels were retained. Taking the present efficiency and specific coal consumption of the existing engine it was calculated that 10½ tons instead of the present 7 tons of coal would be required from London to Glasgow—something like 4 shovels per minute. To retain a moderate combustion rate of 50 lbs. per sq. ft. of grate per hour a grate area of 70 sq. ft. was necessary, and mechanical stoking essential. To produce 30% increase in tractive effort at 60 m.p.h. 4-cylinders 17½″ × 28″ were chosen with a boiler pressure of 300 lbs. per sq. in. The 56,000 lbs. starting Tractive effort which this would normally allow was limited to 42,800 lbs. by fixing the maximum cut-off at 65%.

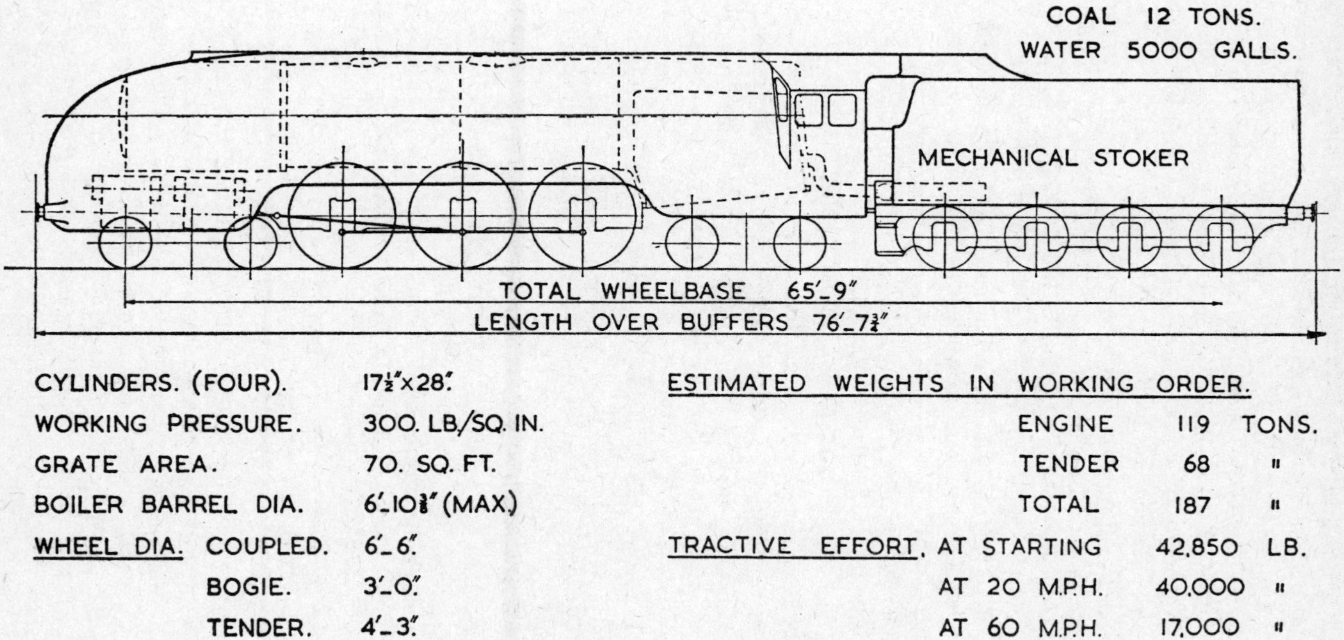

PROPOSED LARGE PASSENGER LOCOMOTIVE

Fig. 23

The kernel of the problem was to find sufficient boiler capacity, which depended upon getting enough total free area through the tube bank. To do this, following the precedent of the German standard engines, the combustion chamber was eliminated, and by reverting to 6′ 6″ diameter coupled wheels an outside boiler diameter of 6′ 10⅜″ at the firebox end was attainable within the loading gauge. This permitted a total tube-free area of 9.8 sq. ft., or 14% of the grate area which was considered just acceptable. The tubes were to be 20′ 6″ long and the firebox 10′ long by 8′ 6″ wide outside. To support the back end a bar frame was proposed from the coupled wheels rearward, or even bar frames throughout, and a trailing bogie. The total engine weight was estimated at 119 tons, with an axle weight of 24 tons which it was thought might be obtainable from the civil engineers, having regard to absence of hammerblow and the fact that the Turbomotive was already running with 23 tons. A four-axle rigid wheelbase tender brought up the rear with capacity for 12 tons of coal and 5,000 gallons of water, pickup gear permitting a total consumption of nearly 20,000 gallons for the trip. Streamlining was retained because at the higher sustained speeds even the few hundred h.p. which it would give was thought worth having. Engine and tender together would have weighed 187 tons.

In contemplating this noble design in retrospect it had every chance of success in performance and steam producing capacity. We know now that the stoker would have lowered efficiency somewhat due to the 'Fines' blown away up the chimney, and some increase in tender coal capacity might have been needed. Cylinders, valve gear, bearings, front end, and steam producing capacity all seemed assured, and the only sensitive spot lay in the capacity of the ashpan. Unless this could be designed to contain the ash dropped from the burning of 10 to 12 tons of coal, without building up so high as to interfere with air flow under the grate, then a non-stop run to Glasgow was impossible. Service stops for ash disposal on the American pattern would destroy the *raison d'être* for the locomotive. I do not think a solution was impossible, but great ingenuity would have been needed to attain it.

The development work of these last two years before the war now veered away from the making of new designs towards improving the existing breed. An account has already been given of the better understanding of boiler proportions which stemmed from the work of R. P. Wagner of the German Reichsbahn. Early in 1938 the publication of Chapelon's mighty book

La Locomotive à Vapeur[1] directed attention throughout the world to the value of opening out the steam circuit all the way from regulator to blast-pipe tip, and of effecting the greatest possible measure of internal streamlining. These lessons were applied to simple expansion on the L.M.S. by improvement in valve head shapes, and ports and passages in the cylinders. A lot of investigation was undertaken on the relation between piston head and cylinder since wear at this point continued as a major problem of the reciprocating engine. Design, materials and lubrication were considered. Piston rod packing was another weak spot, at which white metal alloy had given way to the Western impregnated asbestos 'rope' packing. This proving unsatisfactory left the field for the alternatives of cast-iron segmental rings, nurtured originally on the old North Stafford, and copper-lead alloy rings, an importation from the U.S.A. A bitter war was waged between the protagonists of each, neither in fact fully solving the problem. It was after Stanier's time when cast iron finally won the day, and drop grates, hopper ashpans and self-cleaning smokeboxes were adopted. More heroically, the Lamont forced circulation principle, previously referred to in connection with the Turbine-Electric project, was now reconsidered in the form of a water-tube firebox for the Class 5 4–6–0; rather understandably nobody had the courage to proceed with so drastic a scheme.

In 1939 there was a general stocktaking of progress up to that time as a result of a drive to lower coal consumption. A total amount of 5,785,000 tons burned on locomotives in 1925, had become reduced to 5,358,000 tons in 1939. Although total traffic had declined, overall speed had increased, and the difference was largely due to improvements in the locomotives themselves. For example, 56% of the stock was now superheated instead of 18% in 1923; 25% had 200 lbs. boiler pressure or above against 0.5%; 26% had long-travel valve gear against 0.2%, and 28% had narrow ring valves where there were none originally. It was estimated that if and when these features permeated the whole of the stock, a total of 4 million tons per annum would suffice. This goal was painfully slow in arriving due to limitation in capital expenditure on renewals and major rebuilds. It was, however, decided to press on after improved efficiency. Irrespective of the 4–6–4, which was an exercise in increased power, a proposal was initiated to build two more standard 'Pacifics' in 1940. These were to have 300 lbs. per sq. in. boiler pressure, a 'Houlet' type superheater to

[1] *La Locomotive à Vapeur*—A. Chapelon (J. B. Baillière & Fils, Paris, 1938).

give 750°F. steam temperature, separate headers for saturated and superheated steam, also greatly enlarged steam pipe diameter, steam chest volume and piston valve size and $1\frac{3}{4}''$ steam lap. It was intended to obtain a higher level of steam production by use of Kylchap double blast pipe, in conjunction with more small tubes of lesser diameter, and arch tubes or thermic syphons in the firebox.

Apart from the locomotive proper, it was in this period that the Hudd system of Automatic Train Control was developed to reality, and a great deal of preliminary work was done on a high-speed vacuum brake. This device automatically applied brake block pressure in proportion to speed.

A large part of my time in 1938 and 1939 was spent in preparing for, serving on, and compiling the subsequent report of the Indian Pacific Locomotive Committee, a full account of which is given in the second volume of this book. Suffice it to say here that this enquiry shed a lot of oblique light upon the British locomotive scene, where hitherto many of the factors affecting riding of locomotives as vehicles on the track had been ill understood. Unexplained happenings, such as the derailment of a Royal Scot at Weaver Junction in 1930, and those of a 2–6–4 Tank and of a 'Lord Nelson' on the Southern Railway in 1927 and 1930 respectively, now began to fall into a pattern in which insufficient or ineffective lateral control at bogie and truck played a large part. A general increase in the value of bogie side controls on large engines, from as little as 1 ton up to the region of 4 tons, was undertaken. Gelson and Blackwood, who had produced a lateral force recording apparatus for the Indian Railway Board which had been so useful in illuminating the problem before the enquiry, were now seconded on loan to the L.M.S. and worked out a similar apparatus for us.

In these years electrification remained quiescent, although the appointment of C. E. Fairburn from the English Electric Co. as Chief Electrical Engineer in 1934, and as Deputy C.M.E. in 1937, foreshadowed some awakening in this long dormant form of traction. On the diesel front nothing matured, or was even contemplated, for mainline service, but for shunting some lasting development was undertaken which will be referred to in the next chapter.

In June 1939 the whole C.M.E. department was moved back to Derby. Throughout the history of the large groups, and subsequently into Nationalisation, the C.M.E. has always been at the wrong end. If he was adjacent to his main workshops management

Table VIII. Development of Stanier locomotives (1932-1935)

Power Class	Wheel Arrgt.	Euston Diagram No.	Date of Diagram	Cylinders Dia. × Stroke	Coupled Wheels Dia.	Boiler Pressure lbs./sq. in.	Tractive Effort lbs.	Maximum Axle Weight T. C.	Total Engine Weight T. C.	Comments	First Built	Fig. No.
7	4–6–2	EU.8	4/32	(3) 19 × 28	6′ 9″	250	39700	22.10	104.10	Stovepipe Chimney	—	18
		EU.12	4/32	(4) 16½ × 28	6′ 9″	250	40000	22.10	104.10	Stovepipe Chimney	—	
		EU.12 amended	—	(4) 16¼ × 28	6′ 6″	250	40000	22.10	104.10	Caledonian Chimney	1933	—
5X	4–6–0	EU.32	6/32	(3) 17 × 26	6′ 9″	225	26600	—	—	Taper Boiler on existing 5X Chassis	1934	—
5	4–6–0	DD.2159	3/32	(3) 15½ × 28	6′ 0″	225	26800	—	—	Sloping throatplate 14′ Tubes	—	20
		EU.34	6/32	(3) 15½ × 28	6′ 0″	225	26800	—	—	Vertical throatplate 14′ 9″ Tubes	—	—
		EU.44	7/32	(2) 18½ × 28	6′ 0″	225	25500	18.19	74.18	2-cylinder version of above	1934	—
5	2–6–0	EU.13	4/32	(2) 18 × 28	5′ 6″	225	26400	18.10	65. 0	Stovepipe Chimney 12′ 3″ Tubes	1933	19
4	4–6–0	EU.209	1933	(2) 18 × 28	5′ 6″	200	23400	15.15	63.15	For Scotland	Not Built	22
8	2–8–0	DD.2159	3/32	(3) 15½ × 28	4′ 8½″	225	34100	—	—	Sloping Throatplate 14′ Tubes	—	—
		EU.45	7/32	(2) 18½ × 28	4′ 8½″	225	32600	16.10	72. 0	Vertical Throatplate 14′ 9″ Tubes	1935	21
4	2–6–2T	EU.22	3/32	(3) 16 × 26	5′ 9″	200	24600	19. 0	84. 0	For Tilbury Line. Fowler Cab.	—	—
	2–6–4T	EU.88	11/32	(3) 16 × 26	5′ 9″	200	24600	19.10	91.10	For Tilbury Line. Single Window Cab	1934	—
	—	—	1934	(2) 19⅝ × 26	5′ 9″	200	24670	18. 0	88. 0	2-cylinder version of above	1935	—
3	2–6–2T	—	1932	(2) 17½ × 26	5′ 3″	200	21456	—	—	Taper Boiler on existing Chassis	1935	—

Table IX. New steam locomotives added to L.M.S. stock during eight years 1932-1939 (incl.)

			1932	*1933*	*1934*	*1935*	*1936*	*1937*	*1938*	*1939*	*Total*
Pre-Stanier Designs											
Class 5X	4–6–0	3 cyl. (Parallel Boiler)	15	25	10	—	—	—	—	—	50
4	4–4–0	3 cyl. Compound	5	—	—	—	—	—	—	—	5
2	4–4–0	2 cyl.	35	—	—	—	—	—	—	—	35
4	2–6–4	'Fowler' Tank	10	39	1	—	—	—	—	—	50
3	2–6–2	'Fowler' Tank	10	—	—	—	—	—	—	—	10
2	0–4–4	'Lemon' Modified Tank	9	1	—	—	—	—	—	—	10
7	0–8–0	Freight Tender	40	—	—	—	—	—	—	—	40
5	2–6–0	Horwich Mixed Traffic	10	—	—	—	—	—	—	—	10
4	0–6–0	Supr. Freight	—	—	—	—	—	15	—	20	35
0	0–4–0	'Lemon' Modified Saddle Tank	5	—	—	—	—	—	—	—	5
		Total Pre-Stanier	139	65	11	—	—	15	—	20	250
Stanier Designs											
Class 7	4–6–2	Princess Royal	—	2	—	10	—	—	—	—	12
7	4–6–2	Turbomotive	—	—	—	1	—	—	—	—	1
7	4–6–2	Coronation	—	—	—	—	—	5	10	5	20
6	4–6–0	3 cyl. Rebuilt Scot (No. 6170)	—	—	—	1	—	—	—	—	1
5X	4–6–0	3 cyl. Taper Boiler	—	—	90	40	61	—	—	—	191
5	4–6–0	2 cyl. Mixed Traffic	—	—	46	179	74	153	20	—	472
4	2–6–4	3 cyl. 'Tilbury' Tank	—	—	37	—	—	—	—	—	37
4	2–6–4	2 cyl. Taper Boiler Tank	—	—	—	8	116	27	34	1	186
3	2–6–2	2 cyl. Taper Boiler Tank	—	—	—	74	—	39	26	—	139
5	2–6–0	2 cyl. Taper Boiler Mixed Traffic	—	15	25	—	—	—	—	—	40
8	2–8–0	2 cyl. Freight	—	—	—	12	57	27	2	28	126
		Total Stanier	—	17	198	325	308	251	92	34	1225
		Grand Total	139	82	209	325	308	266	92	54	1475

complained that he was too far away to assist with policy decisions; if at Headquarters he was too far away from the workshops, which languished in all kinds of ways without his personal and direct control. There has never been any real solution of this dilemma. On this occasion, as far as it was possible to find out, the move was occasioned fifty-fifty by the chief's wish to be stationed at one of his works, and management's wish to disperse its forces against the impending war. The whole work force, men, women and office boys, some 200 strong took possession of a gaunt, bleak, and hitherto only partly used building in Nelson Street near Derby Station, and accommodated themselves as best they could to its cavernous depths. Stanier had no sooner had his new office furnished than he was required to return south again—his presence there had become essential when war broke out in September. Thus ended a phase in all our lives, a phase in which it hardly occurred to anyone on our railway to question the supremacy of steam, except only that thwarted and disillusioned rump, left over from the brilliant dawn of O'Brien, which had perforce to content itself with the problems of minor suburban lines. The thought that one day the cream of all the L.M.S. mainline traffic would be drawn by an agency which was neither steam nor straight electric, was as remote from our minds as that man could one day navigate the stratosphere.

VI

The War Years and After

1940-1947

NOTHING today makes such dry reading as those voluminous records, collected by industrial concerns immediately after the close of hostilities, chronicling all that their staffs and workshops contributed to the war effort. Desperately vital as they had been for our survival, the world has moved on since then and little of it is relevant or even interesting to us now. If they are mentioned in this chapter it is in the context of the sub-theme of the author's own experiences.

On the other hand, locomotives, and the men to produce them and make them go, were needed in war as in peace, so there is still something to record as our story enters the nineteen-forties and reaches in 1945 the end of the war, and, two years later, the end of the L.M.S. Railway itself. There were, as a matter of fact, five quite clearly defined, even if overlapping, stages in our activities in the Chief Mechanical Engineer's Department which I will mention together now, before dealing with each in turn.

Firstly, from mid-1939 into 1940, when the department had returned to Derby, there was the run down and putting into cold storage of locomotive design and development. From 1940 to almost exactly half way through the war in mid-1942 there was the utmost pressure to spare as many men and workshop facilities as possible for Government work, guns, tanks, aircraft, etc., coupled with the maximum of make-do and mend with the existing rolling stock. From mid-1942 until the end of the war, with the opening up of Middle Eastern and eventually the second fronts, there was equal and opposite pressure to get the Government work out of the railway workshops again. They needed to combine all their resources for the maximum building and repair of locomotives and wagons required to fill the transport needs of the expanding armies. In the fourth stage in 1944-1945 was the gradual re-awakening of interest in locomotive design and development, in anticipation of the end of the war. Finally 1946 and 1947 were the first years of peace with their opportunities and their uncertainties.

Plate 43. Stanier taper boiler Class 3 2–6–2T works a down suburban train near Radlett.

Plate 44. Fairburn 2–6–4T No. 42250 approaches Amersham with a London Transport Aylesbury-Baker Street train.

Plate 45. Ivatt class 2 2–6–0 mixed traffic engine No. 46502 stands at Derby.

Plate 46. Ivatt class 2 2–6–2T No. 41284 propels the Chesham branch train out of Chalfont & Latimer.

Plate 47. A full-size wooden model of an Ivatt 2–6–2 tank.

Plate 48. Intermediate proposal for the Class 4 2–6–0, 1944.

For better understanding of what follows a few words on organisation cannot be avoided. From the first day of the war all British Railways were unified under the Railway Executive Committee, consisting of the General Managers of the four main line companies plus London Transport. The remit was very simple—" to operate the railways as one unit to the best advantage, and to give the greatest possible assistance to the Government ". Rolling stock and workshop matters were handled by a Mechanical and Electrical Engineers' Committee consisting of the C.M.E.'s, and C.E.E.'s where they existed, of each of the five railways.

To handle all the multiple problems affecting his department between the L.M.S. management, Railway Executive and the Government Departments, Stanier at once set up an office at the 'Grove', near Watford, to which the bulk of the L.M.S. management staff had been evacuated from Euston. Here his time was fully occupied on inter-railway and policy matters with the various bodies still functioning in London. Mechanical engineering proper on the L.M.S. was now in the hands of Fairburn, whose office remained at Derby, and whose principal assistants were Ivatt, Harper and Pugson for Locomotive, Electrical and Carriage and Wagon matters respectively. The various proposals outlined in the last chapter towards 'doing a Chapelon' on the next lot of Pacifics were now laid aside 'for the duration' together with the Mobile Testing Units, the Flange Force Testing apparatus and all the plans for Rugby Testing Station. The Amsler equipment for the new Dynamometer Car just scraped home from Switzerland in one of the last ferry vans to get through, and was greased and stored.

A residue of the older draughtsmen under Coleman continued quietly with the various locomotive modifications which war service required. In between times they did a certain amount of 'doodling' by way of diagrams for future locomotives, as will presently be seen.

Top priority at Derby was a drive to get war work into the main workshops. This was so effective that by the autumn of 1940 the L.M.S. was using as many weekly manhours on direct Government work as were the whole of the other British Railways put together. This was helped by the initiation by Ivatt, some time before the war, of Tank Design and Construction, and by the unrelenting drive on the part of Fairburn and Pugson for the introduction of aircraft work into the carriage works. Second priority was to squeeze out the maximum number of serviceable locomotives which the above activity made possible, by introducing measures to reduce the number under and awaiting repair, to retain in traffic engines already condemned to be broken up, and by drastically reducing further breaking-up programmes. By mid-1941 over 500 additional engines were in traffic as a result. The manhour content of each repair was reduced by relaxation of repair limits and reduction in standard of finish where it was not vital, while materials requirements were eased by use of British Standards instead of the more stringent L.M.S. specifications, and also by an increased use of second-hand material. None of these measures were ideal, but only by such means was it possible, two years after the war began, to spend 21% of the total workshop wages on war work, and carry out the required engine repairs with only 1.3% increase in total staff over pre-war. The third major activity was to meet the insatiable demands for information and action which poured in from the Railway Executive Committee via the L.M.S. management, and via Stanier by reason of his membership of the M. & E.E.'s Committee. Endless appreciations of the locomotive stock position had to be prepared, forecasts of iron, steel and non-ferrous requirements made, and accounts given of supply of locomotives for overseas, staff for war work and dilution with female labour were only a few of the headings.

In my continuing capacity as Personal and Technical Assistant I remained at Derby until early in 1941, increasingly engrossed in the last two of these three activities. It was now that my spell in the workshops in the mid-thirties stood me in such good stead, and I did not find indigestible my daily diet of repair outputs, manhours, machine loadings and staff statistics. My regular attendance at the monthly works superintendents' meetings, chaired by Fairburn, kept me in close touch with all of these interrelated activities.

There were seven main workshops on the L.M. of which Crewe, Derby, Horwich and St. Rollox, managed respectively by F. A. Lemon, Rankin, Williamson and Bond, dealt with locomotives. The other Derby works and those at Wolverton and Earlestown, with Pugson, Peters and Anthony respectively in charge covered carriages and wagons. Two years after the outbreak of war Bond replaced Lemon at Crewe when the latter retired.

On Gresley's death, in April 1941, Stanier took over the chairmanship of the M. & E.E.'s Committee. Almost at the same time the continuing extreme unevenness of the war work effort being made by the different railways caused a committee on the use of Railway Workshops for Government work to be set up under the

Ministry of War Transport. Sir Alan Mount, Chief Inspecting Officer of Railways, previously referred to in connection with the Indian Pacific Locomotive Enquiry, was appointed to the chair, and membership consisted of each railway C.M.E. plus representatives from the Ministries of Supply, Aircraft Production and Labour, together with the Admiralty.

To help cope with all this Stanier now had me transferred to him personally at the London end for four days a week. The 'Grove' was a singularly unattractive brick-built mansion standing in its own grounds about two miles north of Watford. It seemed to have been designed for 'my lord and his lady' in the few spacious rooms downstairs, and for a retinue of some fifty or so servants who must have inhabited the warren of low tiny rooms which occupied most of the upstairs. I found myself occupying a desk opposite Stanier in a low-ceilinged back bedroom, with two clerks working behind a lath and plaster partition. As the building had had to be occupied at minimum expenditure the atmosphere was austere with whitewood furniture, rickety stairs, creaking uncovered floor boards, and tortuous passages—so very different from the eventual splendour when long afterwards the place was gutted and transformed into the Work Study Training Centre for British Railways. But it was an honour indeed to be inside the main building at all. Rudguard, in charge of Motive Power, lived in an ex-stable, and the *hoi polloi* were squeezed, a hundred at a time, into army-type wooden huts scattered over the grounds in the immediate vicinity.

For the remaining two working days I returned to Derby and acted as liaison between all of the interconnected activities of the two centres. To equate with these increased responsibilities I was now appointed Chief Technical Assistant, and was happy in that to become Chief anything was a satisfying step in the right direction. For this I received another £100 bringing me up to a salary of £800. However, I could not help but observe, somewhat wryly, that the previous holder of this title, Hornbuckle, who had just retired, got £1,500, while Herbert Chambers's job, worth another £1,200, had already been merged with my own after his premature death. Such were the ways of the old staff people, the rate for the job was just not in them, and aspirants for further promotion, if wise, kept their thoughts to themselves. It was enough to realise that one was on the way up at last.

I now had to walk the tightrope of coping with the highly varying personal characteristics of Stanier, Fairburn and Ivatt, and also for the first time came into continuous contact with the C.M.E.'s of the other railways and their leading henchmen.

Three more different men than the above named would be hard to find, differing as widely in their backgrounds as in their characters. Ivatt was that rare type, the truly instinctive engineer who had a flair for arriving at effective action with a minimum of intermediate thought processes or paper work. Son of a famous C.M.E. and occupying throughout his career the inside curve of the track as regards familiarity with the railway heirachy, he maintained an effortless efficiency in attaining maximum results with a minimum of effort or fuss. He valued word of mouth communication from his staff, and looked coldly upon all but the briefest and most essential of reports and memos. He was apt to blow people out of his office who came in with letters for signature after 4 p.m. and to chase others off the premises who felt the need to work beyond 5.30 p.m. He was indeed a kindly martinet in reverse, so different from those who only seemed to measure worth by the willingness to make a display of long hours, and all the time leading his staff towards his own ideal of greater effectiveness by cutting down unnecessary pother. Due to this, eager beavers sometimes thought him lazy, but such was far from being the case, for it could not be denied that he was as successful in all he undertook as any who criticised him.

Fairburn, on the other hand, was one of the first examples of someone coming straight from outside industry into a top position in railway engineering. Starting as Chief Electrical Engineer in 1934, he was far from being solely an electrician, and his former positions of responsibility with the English Electric Co., including their heavy mechanical engineering activities, gave him great authority in dealing with railway workshops and production matters after he became Deputy C.M.E. Thus he was a scourge of the inefficient in the shops, and soon became extremely 'canny' in weighing up form on steam traction matters, in which, to the surprise of some and the affront of others, he took a very real interest. A protégé of Sir Harold Hartley, who was his strong supporter at management level, he had a brain like a calculating machine, and liked to arrive at all his results by the operation of pure logic. For this, unlike Ivatt, he called for the utmost by way of detailed and accurate information, not only because whole segments of railway activity were new to him, but also because that was the way he liked it—he was prepared to take endless time and trouble with the job in hand, and to give it his undivided attention, and he expected his staff to do the same.

Thus it was not surprising that it required not a little finesse to satisfy Fairburn and Ivatt simultaneously, and to interpret Stanier's activities and demands to both, in a manner which did not fall foul of the susceptibilities of any of the three of them. Occasionally it took some doing to avoid this undesirable outcome since their admiration for one another's ways was not always boundless.

Mount's committee waged a ceaseless war of nerves on the C.M.E.'s and Sir Alan used the techniques of his former enquiries into train accidents to conduct inquisitions into everything which prevented or delayed increase in Government work in railway shops. I attended this body with Stanier at its fortnightly meetings, and because of our old association on the Indian trip, and because in true civil service style Mount was expected to be fully effective with no other help than his excellent secretary, Miss Moll, it fell to my lot to do a great deal of devilling work for him as well. In the next twelve months I visited most of the workshops of the L.N.E., W. and S. Railways, and did a lot of spadework connecting the capacity which these centres could generate with the kind of work which was suitable from Ministry of Supply, Ministry of Aircraft Production and Admiralty. By October 1941 it had to be reported to the Minister of War Transport that war work in railway shops had reached the point where supply of labour was the controlling factor, and the battle then veered more in the direction of labour supply, dilution of skilled work by semi-skilled and unskilled operatives, and the employment of women.

By March 1942 the first rumbles were heard of shortages of locomotives to cope with the enormously increasing war traffic, and in June the R.E.C. had to report that it was 500 locomotives short to deal even with the traffic in hand, to say nothing of what was yet to come both at home and abroad. Now all our activities were thrown into reverse and within a month or two Mount and his committee was exerting as much pressure to get all war work out of the workshops which could in any way impede production of locomotives and wagons. The companies were only permitted to build mixed traffic or freight engines, and it was now decided that only one class of the latter, the L.M.S. Stanier 2–8–0 should be built as a single standard by all railways. This meant building this type at Doncaster, Swindon, and even Brighton, and a lot of new machine tools were made available to increase production, especially at Brighton, where brand new building capacity was created after a lapse of many years. New building by the railways, which had fallen to 2 per week for all companies, was now to be built up towards the full capacity of 10 per week.

With the possibility of a second front at last, numbers of locomotives far beyond the capacity of the railway shops would be required and it was towards the end of 1942 that Riddles, seconded away from the L.M.S. since September 1939 as Deputy Director General, Royal Engineer Equipment, re-entered the locomotive scene in a dramatic way. Large orders for new engines were to be placed on the private locomotive builders, and to get maximum output the Stanier 2–8–0 was taken in hand. Under Riddles' guidance, using the drawing offices of the builders, every feature was so scrutinised for ease and economy of manufacture that what was really an entirely new design emerged with round top parallel boiler instead of Belpaire taper, with cast iron instead of cast steel wheel centres, and a host of other substitutions and simplifications to produce the now well-known W.D. austerity class.

Stanier was a little bit huffy about all this as he thought too much had been sacrificed to assure economical operation. However, his own design remained unchanged for the railway build, and the 20% saving in production man hours of the W.D. engine just could not be gainsaid in the big drive which was now necessary for the overseas war effort.

In November 1942 the first imports of American built 2–8–0's destined for the second front reached England, and within 9 months 390 of them were in the country and many were put to work and formed a novel sight in British surroundings. For working here they needed certain alterations such as equipping them with a steam brake and fitting a tender hand-brake. I had a few rides on these engines which were well liked by our drivers because they steamed excellently and pulled hard. On the other hand their cabs were rather caves of the winds, and the steam brake which was fitted was distinctly poor for unfitted train working. They were designed and built of course to use the air brake.

By 1943 labour supply was becoming critical and I was made member of a special sub-committee formed to keep this side under continuous scrutiny. The climax was reached when a working party was set up to stump the country to gather in every boilermaker who could hold a hammer, these gentlemen being the real bottleneck. Whittle of the Ministry of Supply was our leader, an 'original' who, before the war, had challenged the monopoly of the great Superheater Co. by setting up his own manufacture of elements at Eccles. J. M. D. Wrench, who had been Controller of Standardisation during our visit to India in 1938, represented the Ministry of Supply and Cdr. Rose-Killey, retd., was on for the Admiralty. This was I think the most exhaustive mission I have ever been on, in which we visited every locomotive workshop, large or small, railway or private, in the country, together with shipyards and other non-railway employments into which our boilermakers had been drafted or filtered of their own accord. Name by name and man by man 349 boilermakers were identified as suitable for return, and the Ministry of Labour then set to work and succeeded in winkling out a major proportion from wherever they were. The final stages of the Mount Committee and whole subject of railway war work were reached in September 1944 when criticisms actually reached us from on high that we were retaining too much Government work—irony indeed! Existing contracts, mainly aircraft, had still to be honoured, but there were now only one-third of the staff remaining, as compared with the number employed on Govermnent work at the height of Mount's original drive. Moreover, of these many were women who were not in general suitable for railway work.

The Mechanical and Electrical Engineers' Committee also met once a fortnight throughout the war, and dealt with everything remitted to it by the R.E.C. From Stanier's taking of the chair I had to attend every meeting as his dogsbody and to do all the technical devilling beforehand, also act as go-between with Fairburn and Ivatt in what affected the L.M.S. Stanier made an urbane and unflappable chairman and he needed all his phlegm for he had some spirited members to control. Bulleid of the Southern, wayward then as ever, was not to be prevented by any war from producing his *magnum opus*, and the first 'Merchant Navy' came out in March 1941, right in the middle of the frantic drive to replace locomotive building by military production. Worse still it was clearly an express passenger engine notwithstanding its author's protestations that it counted as a mixed traffic. There were dark mutterings from high places that he ought to be stopped, but he nevertheless succeeded in producing 17 of them before the war ended. Hawkesworth was a true son of Swindon, a master of uncommunication. Swindon had never been used to giving out, and although the new C.M.E. was a loyal member of the team, who caused great efforts to be produced by his workshops, one always had to work hard to get information out of him as little was volunteered. Hawkesworth's *gethsemanes* were the Mount meetings where his spirit groaned aloud in the frustration of being alternatively bullied and coaxed to produce, to him, quite meaningless data.

Another new boy was Edward Thompson who had succeeded Gresley in 1941. He was a most imposing figure, tall, aristocratic looking, immaculately dressed, whose wont at the beginning of a meeting was to set out on the table before him an assortment of gold pencils, chains, watches and other symbols of well-being. Although he played his full part in all that was going on, another part of his mind was clearly occupied by thoughts of the locomotives he was going to design, and the name he was going to make for himself in correcting the mistakes of his predecessor, as he clearly thought them to be. He had a considerable admiration for Stanier, and used to discuss with him, and even with me, the various projects he had in mind, the most effective and successful of which was the B1 class 4–6–0, conceived to play the same role on the L.N.E. as as the Class 5 did on the L.M.S. This association led to an intensely interesting diversion in 1942 when he arranged with Stanier for me to visit Doncaster and prepare a report on the 2 to 1 valve gear. This was a Gresley feature which he particularly disliked and which, under wartime conditions of maintenance, was giving a lot of trouble. I could not, of course, report upon what it had been like in the heyday of the A4's pre-war. However, it was unassailable fact that unit play at each of the eight pin joints was multiplied by eleven by the time that it reached the middle valve, and in fully rundown condition the lost motion could amount to $\frac{3}{8}''$. This resulted in reduced power at low speeds due to insufficient port opening, while at high speed the combined effect of overtravel of the valve, plus whip in the combining levers, could produce up to 50% more power in the inside cylinder than in either of the outside. There was also a spate of hot inside big-ends, ten times as many in the inside position as at the outside, six times as many as the L.M. experienced with the inside big-ends on a comparable number of its own 3-cylinder engines. A certain lack of stiffness in the marine big-end arrangement also appeared to contribute to this result. All this, of course, was only saying what Thompson could perfectly say for himself, but he no doubt used the final report over Stanier's signature to full effect with his directors in the Machiavellian campaign he was conducting against all things Gresley.

At this time all the donkey work for Thompson on the M.E. and

Mount Committees was being done for him by Harry Harper and Jimmy Blair whom I came to know very well, and in Thompson's absence a massive and most urbane individual came as figurehead, A. H. Peppercorn, Assistant C.M.E. 'Pep' as he was usually called seemed to be loved by all, and his contributions kept closely to his prepared brief. Not for him were any excursions into the mental stratosphere, but if he himself was not a very live wire he had the inestimable ability of letting his assistants get on with it, and when Thompson retired after the war and 'Pep' himself succeeded to the position, he reversed a lot of his predecessors' high-handed actions and encouraged a resumption of locomotive practice more in the Gresley tradition. He was powerfully aided in this by his new assistant Freddie Harrison, a name appearing for the first but not the last time in this chronicle.

Besides locomotive matters coming up at this Committee, and the many others which were ever present in running the L.M.S., a certain amount of extra-mural professional activity continued in the Institutions, which early in the war were able to resume their meetings albeit on a muted scale. Although I had qualified for parts A and B of the Institution of Mechanical Engineers entry examination, by the Higher National Certificate I had gained at Manchester, I had done no more about it, until Stanier—as President elect—urged me to send in my entry papers. It was no doubt through his influence on the Council that I was elected Associate Member in early 1941, without further examination. It is thought by many a cowardly way to enter the Institutions, by waiting until one's job status permits painless infiltration in this manner, and much merit attaches to those who take their full exams and climb the hard way. I, myself, have never felt any pangs of conscience because almost at once I became involved in the production of a paper and thus sang for my supper in a manner of speaking.

When Stanier and I had visited India in 1938 H. N. Colam, then C.C.E. of the M. & S.M. Railway, had been conducting a lot of experiments on locomotives having nil reciprocating balance. He returned to England, and now as Sir Harold Colam, he had prepared a paper for the Institution of Civil Engineers entitled "Hammer Blow in Locomotives, Can It Not Be Abolished Altogether?" In Stanier's Presidential year the Mechanicals were looking for a companion paper, giving the other side, for presentation at a joint meeting of the two Institutions and the task fell to my lot. My long train journeys about the country, in deeply shaded light then obligatory, were occupied by much scribbling, and for the first time I was able to draw freely upon technical data from the other railways. I shall have something to say on the technical aspects of this debatable theme in the next volume, but here I would only comment that the two papers were given on December 16th, 1941, and it turned out to be quite an evening. My paper was published in the journals of three Institutions, the Locomotive Engineers being the third, and in due course I was awarded the George Stephenson Research Prize by the Mechanicals. It would be churlish not to feel rather pleased with oneself after all that, and I did think that I had rather earned my entry after all.

We now come to the gradual re-awakening of interest in locomotive development which began in 1944 and which looked increasingly towards what was to be done at the onset of peace. There had been an important change at the end of 1942 when Stanier, whilst still retaining his Chairmanship of the M. & E.E.'s Committee and membership of the Mount Committee, was appointed Scientific Adviser to the Ministry of Production. As such he ceased to be C.M.E. of the L.M.S. and Fairburn was appointed in his place.

Stanier, knighted in January 1943, now worked from a Government office in Whitehall. In mid-1944 he retired as M.E. Chairman and thus finally severed his long and fruitful direct connection with railways, although he lived on to become the greatly honoured *doyen* of British Locomotive Engineers, and is even as I write these lines an alert and interested onlooker upon the doings of the many who have succeeded him.

Fairburn, who became increasingly dogged by ill health, was C.M.E. for three years until his death at the end of 1945. Up to the end of the war he continued to function from Derby with the same team already mentioned. I carried on with the office at the 'Grove', undertaking my former liaison duties at both places, but from October 1944 returned to Derby completely, and it was with some relief that the weekly trek south was at last abated, although plenty of travel remained on committee and other work.

Locomotive activity was brought to life in three forms, namely a new-look at design from the point of view of servicing and maintenance, a modernised version of Stanier's Taper boiler 2–6–4 Tank, and development towards thoroughly up-to-date locomotives for secondary services. War experience had emphasised the deficiencies of existing design in several important directions. Shortage of staff made it increasingly difficult to clean smokeboxes and fires and empty ashpans by the old methods, which were laborious in the extreme, and yet if this work was not properly done performance could be badly affected. It had been fully appreciated pre-war that in U.S. practice these servicing needs were adequately met by the use, in combination, of the self-cleaning smokebox, rocking firegrate and hopper ashpan with bottom doors. These devices have been described[1] and Ivatt now personally sponsored their development and saw to it that they were adapted to L.M.S. design with all that practical flair at which he was so adept.

With the confirmatory experience of the American W.D. locomotives which worked here for some time, and after a few experimental installations on L.M. 4–6–0's and 2–8–0's, these features were applied to all new L.M. construction from 1945 onwards.

The most valuable internal development of this period, however, was the introduction of manganese steel liners in axlebox and horn guide surfaces. The coupled wheel bearing problem has already been traced in these pages from the combination of inadequate size, plus unsuitable design of the pre-grouping days, through the introduction of increased dimensions in Hughes and Fowler's time to Stanier's ultimate improvements which practically banished the hot box once and for all. Axlebox wear and deterioration in service which on the older engines required workshop attention at under 30,000 miles on the average, was now contained sufficiently to double this mileage, with obvious benefit to availability and repair costs. A study made at this time indicated that if the mileage could be raised to 100,000 between successive visits to main works, weekly repair output could be reduced as more engines were brought up to this standard, culminating in a possible saving of a round million pounds per annum if and when the whole stock could be brought into line. Analysis of shopping proposals indicated that it was deterioration in the white metal, with which the axlebox flat surfaces in contact with the horn guides were faced, which so increased play and 'knock' that attention became necessary. Unless better wearing material was found no further progress was possible.

After a number of abortive experiments[2] the attention of Ivatt and his team was turned towards certain American roller bearing applications initiated by the Timken Co. which used unlubricated manganese steel for these flat rubbing surfaces, and the idea of applying this material to plain bearing axleboxes emerged. Trial was made in 1944 on a few Class 5 4–6–0's with quite dramatic

[1] *Master Builders of Steam*—H. A. V. Bulleid (Ian Allan, 1963).
[2] *Locomotive Axleboxes*—E. S. Cox (Journal I.L.E., No. 190, 1944).

results. The first six of these engines to be shopped two years later averaged 83,000 miles, and were brought in not for knock and wear in axleboxes, as formerly, but for other mechanical wear or defects, which now needed closer attention in their turn. The tighter average working clearances which were obtained throughout the shopping life brought ancillary advantages not only in better riding but also in improved mileage between tyre turning due to reduction in the ' quarter slip ' effect.

Less notable but none the less substantial benefits resulted from similar close examination into laminated springs, piston head fixing, piston rod packing, mechanical oil feed direct to underkeeps of coupled axleboxes, and improved frame stays both at the hornblocks and laterally between the frames. In addition, a very large-scale investigation was undertaken into the causes of frame fracture, still epidemic in certain engine classes, and into the re-establishment of limits of wear best suited to the various improvements now coming into being and to the economic conditions of peacetime operation. Thus the L.M.S. engines which were turned out new after the war, although in most cases looking very much the same as before, were in fact tremendously improved in their potential, and were far better fitted to meet the more rugged conditions of the chronic staff shortage which beset locomotive maintenance from this time onwards.

Turning now to the locomotives themselves, as Table XIII shows, there had been a steady building of Stanier 2–8–0's throughout the war, and Class 5 4–6–0's began to appear again from 1943. A small scattered output of 2–6–4 Tanks, assembled from pre-war material already on hand, had continued and it was planned to restart quantity production of these ever useful engines in 1945. Besides applying the various improvements outlined above, Coleman, with Fairburn's encouragement, undertook a considerable general re-design to save weight and material. Retaining the standard taper boiler, the old sacred coupled wheel spacing of 8′ and 8′ 6″, stretching back to Johnson in the last century, was jettisoned. A reduction of 1′ 5″ in total wheelbase, plus a cutting down of the amount of footframing and other redundant details, produced an engine 2 tons 12 cwt. lighter than the previous Stanier Class, and 1 ton lighter than the original Fowler design. No. 2673 was the first out in April 1945, and a total of 130 of these still good-looking engines were built over the last three years of the L.M.S. (Plate 44).

This was the only locomotive to which fate permitted Fairburn's name to be attached. Although he was the first to accept that it

Table X. Development of Classes 2, 3 and 4, 0–6–0 and 2–6–0 engines (1932-1947)

Power Class	*Diagram No.*	*Date*	*Wheel Arrgt.*	*Cylinders Dia. and Stroke*	*Coupled Wheel Dia.*	*Boiler Pressure lbs./sq. in.*	*Tractive Effort lbs.*	*Maximum Axle Weight T. C.*	*Total Engine Weight T. C.*	*Comments*	*First Built*	*Fig. No.*
4	EU.90	12/32	0–6–0	19 × 26	5′ 3″	200	25400			Taper Boiler on existing Fowler Std. Engine		
	DE.48	5/37	2–6–0	18½ × 28	5′ 6″	225	27700	18.16	65.15	Modified version of 2–6–4 Tank		
	DE.51	5/37	2–6–0	18½ × 28	5′ 6″	200	25683	17.10	62. 5	Modified version of 2–6–4 Tank		
	DRS.3518	1937	2–6–0	19⅝ × 26	5′ 9″	200	24670	17.15	62.15	Direct adaption from 2–6–4T		
	DD.3510	1941	0–6–0	18¼ × 26	4′ 11″	200	24530	17.10	50. 2	As first engine above. Raised footplate over rods		
	DD.3681	1943	0–6–0	18½ × 26	4′ 11″	200	25640	17. 2	49. 0	As first engine above. Simplified footplate		
	DD.3688	1943	0–6–0	17½ × 26	4′ 11″	225	25810	—	—	Bar Frames, Wide Firebox, Allen Valve gear, Stovepipe		
	DD.3749	1944	2–6–0	19⅝ × 26	5′ 9″	200	24670	18. 0	62.15	Tender version of Fairburn 2–6–4T. Straight footplate		(PLATE) 48
	As Built	1947	2–6–0	17½ × 26	5′ 3″	225	24172	16.15	59. 2	L.M. No. 3000	1947	
3	DD.3526	1941	0–6–0	17½ × 26	4′ 11″	200	22940	15.13	45.13	As first engine above		
2	EU.390	1934	0–6–0	16½ × 26	5′ 0″	200	20100	15.10	43. 0	Taper Boiler. Inside Walschaerts Normal Footplating		
	DD.3682	1943	0–6–0	16½ × 26	4′ 11″	200	20390	15. 6	44.13	As first engine above		
	DD.2714A	1943	0–6–0	16 × 26	4′ 8½″	200	20030	14. 0	40. 0	} Bar Frame, Wide Firebox, Walschaert Gear		(Fig.) 24
	DD.3711	1943	0–6–0	16½ × 26	4′ 11″	200	20390	15.13	45.13	}		
	DD.3742B	1944	2–6–0	16 × 24	5′ 0″	200	17400	13.10	47. 0	First layout of loco. as finally built		
	DD.3771	1944	0–6–0	16 × 24	5′ 0″	200	17400	15. 7	43. 0	0–6–0 Counterpart of above		
	As Built	1946	2–6–0	16 × 24	5′ 0″	200	17400	13.11	47. 2	L.M. No. 6400	1946	(PLATE) 45

Table XI. Development of Class 2 Tank engines (1934-1946)

Diagram No.	*Date*	*Wheel Arrgt.*	*Cylinders Dia. & Stroke*	*Coupled Wheel Dia.*	*Boiler Pressure lbs./sq. in.*	*Tractive Effort lbs.*	*Maximum Axle Weight T. C.*	*Total Engine Weight T. C.*	*Comments*	*First Built*	*No. Fig.*
EU.391	1934	0–6–2	16½ × 26	5′ 0″	200	20100	16. 0	60. 0	Taper Boiler, inside Walschaert Gear		
DD.3726	1944	2–6–2	16½ × 24	4′ 8½″	200	19660	14.16	63. 0	Alternatives for locomotive as finally built (DD.3726, DD.3726A, DD.3726B)		
DD.3726A	1944	2–6–2	16½ × 26	5′ 0″	200	20100	15. 0	68.10			
DD.3726B	1944	2–6–2	16 × 24	5′ 0″	200	17400	13.15	63. 0			
DD.3735	1944	2–4–2	17½ × 26	5′ 7″	200	20190	19.17	67. 0	Modernised L. & Y. 2–4–2T. Taper Boiler, Inside Cylinders, Stephenson Gear		25
DD.3735A	1944	2–4–2	17 × 26	5′ 6″	200	19350	19. 5	66.10	Two versions of outside cylinder Engine, Walschaert Gear (DD.3735A, DD.3735B)		
DD.3735B	1944	2–4–2	16½ × 26	5′ 6″	200	18240	17.18	65.17			
As Built	1946	2–6–2	16 × 24	5′ 0″	200	17400	15. 5	63. 5	L.M.S. No. 1200	1946	(PLATE) 46

was not his direct inspiration, he nonetheless took much personal interest in its development, and is at least as entitled to have his name given to this particular engine, as were some of his illustrious forebears in office in a similar context.

The third phase of design activity turned out to be the application of all that the preceeding years had taught about locomotives for secondary services, but the initiation of this project stretched backwards over many years. Tables X and XI set out the various steps in this odyssey. By Stanier's advent the continued breaking up of Class 2, 3 and 4 pre-grouping engines, which hitherto worked these services, was beginning to establish the need for new construction in this waveband, which had by no means been wholly satisfied by Fowler's Class 4 0–6–0's and Class 3 2–6–2 Tanks.

Deadlock persisted in translating this need into action, because the motive power people, Urie and Rudguard in particular, wanted straight replacements of the old Class 2 and 3 0–6–0's, saturated boilers, slide valves, the lot. Successive C.M.E.'s and their designers, on the other hand, could not yet again bring themselves only to tinker with the pre-1900 designs, as had been the case with the abortive 0–4–4 Tank in 1931. So nothing was done except the creation and discussion of a lot of engine diagrams from 1932 until 1944, while the battle swung to and fro between inside cylindered front coupled engines, and outside cylindered machines with pony trucks. In the final stage from 1941 onwards, Coleman and his few people still on this kind of work must have got a good deal of amusement out of letting their hair down and in becoming quite uninhibited in what they put down on paper. Bar frames, wide fireboxes, inside Walschaert gear driven from outside return cranks, and stovepipe chimneys were rampant, and to the dustbin with running plates, fall plates, splashers and all the clutter of 100 years of previous design! Fig. 24 indicates an example of what this period produced, and even more fanciful was the tank engine approach shown in Fig. 25 in which some dying embers from Horwich had obviously been stirred fitfully into flames—nothing, it may be said, to do with your author!

These pleasantries over Ivatt was able to exert sufficient mastery over Rudguard's anachronisms, after 1944, to insist that the new engines must be straightforward but thoroughly modern 2–6–0's and 2–6–2 Tanks (Plates 45 and 46). Production design of the Class 2 twins proceeded through 1945, and the first examples were built in 1946 after he had succeeded to the highest office, and they are thus rightly identified with his name. Thus to him goes the credit

POWER CLASSN 2F.

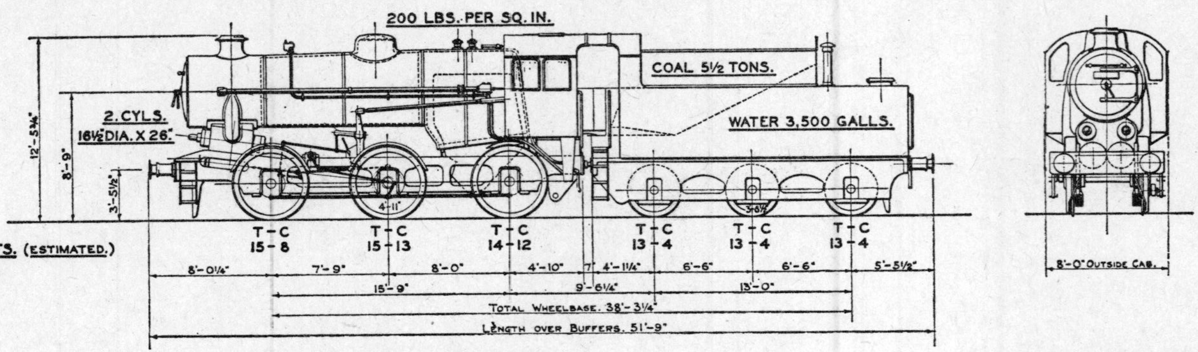

WEIGHTS. (ESTIMATED.)

DESCRIPTION.

BOILER.------------------ OUTSIDE DIA. 4'-6" INCREASING TO 4'-9".
FIREBOX.----------------- OUTSIDE 5'-10" LONG X 5'-6" WIDE.

TUBES.------------------ { SUPERHEATER ELEMENTS 21. 1¼" DIA. OUTS. X 11 S.W.G.
LARGE TUBES. 21. 5⅛" DIA. OUTS. X 7 S.W.G.
SMALL TUBES. 130. 1⅝" DIA. OUTS. X 12 S.W.G. } 10'-10½" BETWEEN TUBEPLATES.

HEATING SURFACE. { TUBES. 908·0 SQ. FT.
FIREBOX. 112·0 " "
SUPERHEATER. 207·0 " " } TOTAL 1,020·0 SQ. FT.

GRATE AREA.------------------------- 25·2 " "
TRACTIVE EFFORT AT 85% B.P. 20,390 LBS.
ADHESION FACTOR. 5·02.

WEIGHTS.

	ENGINE.	TENDER.	TOTAL.
	T-C-Q	T-C-Q	T-C-Q
LIGHT.	41-10-0	18-10-0	60-0-0
LOADED.	45-13-0	39-12-0	85-5-0

RADIUS OF MINIMUM CURVE. }

BRAKE % ENGINE & TENDER. ____________

—— PROPOSED 0-6-0 SUPERHEATED FREIGHT ENGINE. ——

Fig. 24

Plate 49. Caprotti Class 5 4–6–0 No. 44749 approaches Watford with a down train.

Plate 50. The final stage of L.M.S. Class 5 4–6–0 design: No. 44686 with Caprotti valve gear and double chimney.

Plate 51. Rebuilt taper boiler 'Royal Scot' No. 46160 with a down Manchester express near Elstree.

Plate 52. Engines designed by Stanier (48350) Hughes (42897), Fowler (44545), Ivatt (46499), and Fairburn (42053) stand simultaneously in Derby Station in 1957.

Plate 53. The first main line diesel-L.M.S. No. 10000. It is leaving Derby erecting shop on December 8th, 1947, with H. G. Ivatt at the controls.

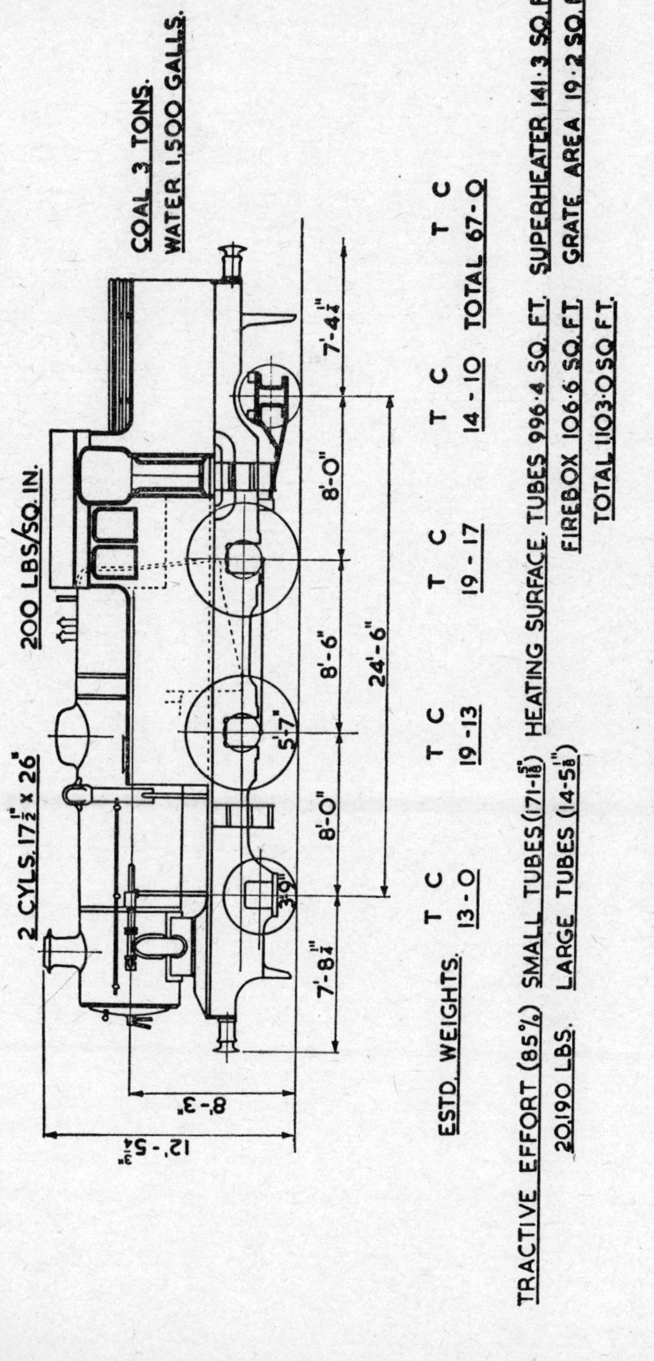

PROPOSED 2-4-2 TANK.

Fig. 25

of producing the only really up-to-date small engines built by any British railway for very many years.

While under design, Fairburn's interest in underwriting all that was being done in the direction of easier servicing in the depots produced an unexpected apparition. So concerned was he with the considerable amount of alteration work which seemed inevitably to follow each new design, that he caused a full-size mock-up of the 2–6–2 Tank to be produced in wood, complete down to the last detail, for inspection and comment by shed staffs. Plate 47 shows this effort which was a good deal jeered at by the old hands. Perhaps it did not cause anything of much moment to be discovered and corrected before the flesh and blood engines were turned out, but on the other hand it only cost £8 for each of the total number of Ivatt Class 2's, which were eventually produced. With all our recent experience with diesels, I am not at all sure to this day that Fairburn did not have something there which might have well justified some further judicious application. Whether originating from this or not, it is a fact that quite large-scale wooden mock-ups have become increasingly used from that time forward.

When the Class 2 designs were frozen, that for a Class 4 2–6–0 had reached the corresponding stage shown in Plate 48, in very presentable form. However, Coleman's wild men set about it again, and when it did appear in 1947, its running plate had shot upwards to the boiler flanks, and it was fitted out with probably one of the ugliest double chimneys ever invented, and one of the most ineffective as it turned out later.

As an epitaph to Fairburn's reign, I recall that coincident with the end of the war in May 1945, he moved down from Derby temporarily to the 'Grove', intending to re-establish himself at Euston with a skeleton technical staff, much as Lemon had done in 1931. I was chosen to go with him, and had just moved my home south from Derby when he died in hospital in October of the same year. I should like to pay a brief tribute to Charles Fairburn, for he is but little regarded now in the historical succession of C.M.E.'s. While circumstances prevented him from doing much on the electrification front it was his drive and persistence which developed the 350 h.p. Diesel-Electric shunter, to such effect that in his lifetime it became a completely effective and trouble-free instrument, and has so remained with little further development up to the present time when 1,400 of these locomotives are at work all over British Railways. In two papers to the Institution of Locomotive Engineers he described in detail the nature of all that was involved in producing this result.[1,2] I enjoyed working with him as much as with any chief before or since, his mind was so quick and receptive. At the same time he had the inestimable capacity of being able to give quite undivided attention to the matter in hand, whatever the pressure of his other pre-occupations. His early demise was a sad end to what was bound to have been an eventful career, for he loved intrigue, and was very cautiously regarded by many of his fellows heads of departments.

In January 1946 Ivatt set up his new post-war C.M.E. organisation at Derby with Roland Bond as Mechanical Engineer (Loco. Works.), later becoming Deputy C.M.E. I was given a very large rise indeed, and while still retaining the same title, was put in charge of Locomotive Design, Development, Testing and the work of the Mechanical Inspection Section, resurrected, in strengthened form, for trouble shooting out in the sheds and on the line. Apart from the maturing of the different matters already described, we all fell to with a will upon a number of further developments now to be described.

The basic Class 5 4–6–0 was tackled, and for the 1947 build, designs were prepared for 20 to have roller bearings on carrying and the coupled axleboxes, some on all such boxes and some on the driving boxes only. Twenty more had these features plus Caprotti valve gear (Plate 49), and the whole 40 were turned out in combinations of single and double blastpipes. One of the first group with double chimney, No. 4767, also had outside Stephenson's valve gear to enable study to be made of the value, if any, of variable lead. Two of the last of this series, Nos. 4686 and 4687, were still further modified with a latest version of the rotary cam poppet valve gear. Not turned out until 1948, these engines had their footplates raised to the level of the boiler flanks. They represented the ultimate departure from the original Stanier design of 1934, and were the forerunners of the B.R. design yet to come (Plate 50). For the 1948 programme more of these engines were planned with steel instead of copper fireboxes, but Nationalisation cut off abruptly any purely L.M.S. innovations.

The last two 4–6–2's turned out in 1947 were also modified to have roller bearings throughout, and as a by-product of equipping them with rocking grates and hopper ashpans were fitted with single extension frames behind the coupled wheels, in conjunction

[1] " Diesel Shunting Locomotion "—C. E. Fairburn (*Proc.* Inst. Loco. Engrs. No. 161, 1941).

[2] " The Maintenance of Diesel-electric Shunting Locomotives on the L.M.S." (*Proc.* Inst. Loco. Engrs. No. 179, 1944).

with cast-steel 'delta' type trailing trucks. These features were part of a drive to raise the annual mileage of these engines from 70,000 to 100,000. It was very appropriate that one of them, No. 6256, was named *Sir William Stanier, F.R.S.*, these letters being only one more distinction which in 1944 fell to the lot of this remarkable man. Here again, it was intended that the 1948 batch should have steel fireboxes and thermic syphons, but this never matured.

The remaining development was the rebuilding of the Royal Scots and of some of the 5X class 4–6–0's with taper boilers, and a wide selection of the other improvements already mentioned. Once more it is necessary to go back a little way to seek the origins. The taper boiler fitted to the Royal Scot No. 6170 in 1935, to replace the unsuccessful Schmidt-Henchel boiler, was unfortunately designed before the various adjustments to the taper 5X boilers were completed, and its tube ratios were far enough astray to make it a rather erratic steamer. The shorter boiler, which was then schemed out in connection with the proposal to convert 5X's to 2-cylinders in 1937, was altogether better proportioned. When under wartime conditions the 5X's, not all of which by any means had been converted to optimum free area and tube ratios, gave further trouble with bad steaming, it was decided to take the bull by the horns and rebuild one of these engines, No. 5736, with this larger boiler carrying 250 lbs. per sq. in. pressure in conjunction with double blast pipe and chimney. This was done in 1942, and a second engine in 1944, which brought performance up from Class 5X to Royal Scot standards, and cured once and for all the steaming problems. The boilers on the 'Scots' themselves were at the war's end approaching twenty years old, and the 'Fowler' type of built-up smokebox became an endless source of air leaks which spoiled the draught, so the decision was made in Fairburn's time to rebuild the whole class on similar lines. This work was well advanced in Ivatt's days, with a few more of the 5X class converted for good measure. Except for a lasting propensity to rough riding,[1] this was undoubtedly the most fully effective and efficient 4–6–0 belonging to any of the group companies (Plate 51). It must be recalled in this connection that the final improvements to the G.W.R. 'Castles' and 'Kings' were not undertaken until after Nationalisation.

Miscellaneous activities in these later years included, of course, the rebirth of locomotive testing, which was from September 1945 onwards controlled by a strong committee consisting of Herbert,

[1] "The Lively 'Royal Scots'"—by '45671' (*Trains Illustrated*—March 1959).

Chief of Research, Bond, Coleman, Pope (Operating) and myself, with Ivatt in the chair. The mobile Testing Units, used as standby power plants in previous years, were refurbished, and the Amsler equipment was released from its cocoon and construction of the new Dynamometer Car pushed ahead. Work on Rugby Testing Station was resumed with Sanford as Superintending Engineer and with a target for opening at the end of 1947, but it was not in fact completed until 1948.

With the stoppage of war contracts the Ministry of Aircraft Production and associated firms were most anxious to find new outlets for Gas Turbine developments. I was teamed with Johansen of the Research Department to report periodically on contacts and developments, none of which were fruitful at this time.

In 1944, 2–10–0 locomotives began running over the Toton to Brent and other lines, a long delayed after-shadow of our efforts back in the ninteen-twenties to produce something similar. These were Riddles' larger W.D. engines having wide steel fireboxes with arch tubes, loaned for home service pending overseas use. Coal shortage loomed up very early after the war, and under Government pressure schemes were demanded from all companies to equip a proportion of their engines for oil firing, and to set up the necessary ground installations. Numbers were in fact put into service, and with careful handling, adequate performance was obtained, but long before the number was considerable the shortage passed, and the uneconomic nature of the exercise became too glaring to continue. With oil at $5\frac{3}{4}$d. per gallon and coal at 40s. 4d. per ton traction cost 1s. 6d. more per engine mile with oil-firing. It was perfectly clear that, if oil fuel had to be used, locomotive fireboxes were not the right place to burn it in this country at any rate.

Before ending this chapter with an account of diesel progress, one or two more personal matters may be mentioned to show the kind of things which occurred in one man's career. At the end of 1944 I nearly left the L.M.S. for a post on the L.N.E.R. Mention has been made of our fortnightly contacts with Edward Thompson, the C.M.E. of the latter, in the course of which I had many discussions and some correspondence with him on design and maintenance matters. In October 1944 he approached me as to whether I would be prepared to come to Doncaster to work under him with the odd title of Mechanical Engineer (Commercial), and on November 15th I was interviewed in his company at King's Cross by the Assistant General Manager. This naturally placed me in something of a dilemma since I was getting along quite nicely on the L.M.S. and liked the people I was working with and for. On the other hand it *was* a step forward in status, with all the possibilities which a new 'milieu' might open up. There were some things, however, which in my innocence I did not, indeed could not, fully appreciate. In the first place I learned many years later that this was one more of Thompson's many internal wars, connected this time with introducing a more central control over maintenance procedure on the L.M.S. model, in the teeth of great opposition from some of his own colleagues. Then again, the genialities of the M. & E.E.'s meetings failed to disclose another side to Thompson's character which was felt in full force by his own assistants and staff, and which resulted in an atmosphere at Doncaster which could hardly be described as that of universal love. In the end, however, the choice was taken out of my hands by Hartley, who, in Fairburn's frequent absences through ill health, did not wish for any disturbances in the Derby team, and who therefore passed the good word along to the L.N.E. management. In idle moments I sometimes wonder what my career would have been had it become diverted into this unpromising channel.

In February 1946 I was elected a member of the Association of Railway Locomotive Engineers—the A.R.L.E., a body which before 1923 had consisted simply of the C.M.E.'s of the different railways, but which had since grouping included some of the senior assistants as well. This organisation operated on two planes—that of intent and that of action—cemented by ample lunches, and in pre-war days by meetings in various delectable spots. The intention was that it should be a forum for joint action towards inter-railway standardisation in mechanical engineering matters. In practice it was a rather equivocal debating society in which few members were prepared to waive their own prerogatives for the common cause. Its only effective measure, which I recall, was the introduction of a standard series of tyre profiles. This had hardly been generally accepted when the G.W.R. broke away, and in characteristic fashion thereafter used one of its own. Nationalisation rather naturally brought the A.R.L.E. to an end. Most tremendous personal adventure of all came in October 1945, when in company with Pugson and Harper, I joined Peppercorn, Richards, and Bramworth of the L.N.E.R. at Southampton and boarded the R.M.S. *Queen Mary* for an exploratory visit to the United States. What we saw and did is referred to at greater length in a later chapter in Volume II.

Reverting to diesel traction it was the depression of the early 1930's which inspired the interest of the L.M.S. management, powerfully influenced by the possibilities of one-man operation, and this railway undoubtedly pioneered locomotive applications in this country. Orders were placed between 1932 and 1934 for 11 diesel shunters as set out in Table XII. Most of them had mechanical transmission with engine power under 200 h.p., but two, having electrical transmission, were above this power. In an exercise which in a curious way forecast what was to happen with main line diesels twelve years later, it was Hornbuckle's idea to obtain samples of everything then available on the market, and after a suitable period of trials, to choose the best for future bulk purchase.[1]

In July 1934, however, Fairburn came over from the English Electric Co. which had provided one out of the trial 11 locomotives. In his new position as Electrical Engineer he immediately took charge of these proceedings, and thereafter only electric drive was considered. It played into his hands that experience in service showed that an engine power of 300–350 h.p. was essential for the intensively worked yards, and electric was the only transmission as yet sufficiently developed for such higher powers. Thus, in 1935, 20 further diesel electrics were ordered, 10 from English Electric and 10 from Armstrong Whitworths. Blood being thicker than water, it was from the former that a standard L.M.S. shunter design was evolved, the first 40 built in 1939 having Jackshaft drive. Thereafter the much more elegant arrangement was worked out of two nose-suspended motors driving the axles direct through double reduction gearing, and 20 of these went into traffic in 1944. By the end of 1945, of these 91 engines, 49, including nearly all the original 200 h.p. mechanical locomotives, had been sold to Ministry of Supply for war work. Two more had been otherwise disposed of, 40 remaining with the L.M.S., 6 of these were to the latest design which, as already mentioned, became the ultimate bulk standard not only for the L.M.S. but eventually for British Railways.

Behind this simple chronicle lay a personal contest between Hornbuckle, the true originator, and Fairburn, who developed these ideas far away from the intentions of their initiator. As a matter of fact, Tommy Hornbuckle was no match, either in position or capacity, for his formidable chief, and before long he retired from

[1] "Application of Diesel Engines to Rail Traction"—T. Hornbuckle (*Proceedings* Diesel Engine Users Assn. 1936).

Table XII. The First Eleven Diesel Locomotives

Locomotive Number	1831	7050	7051	7052	7053	7054	7055 7056	7057	7058	7059
Date	Dec. 1932	Oct. 1934	1932	Jan. 1934	Sep. 1934	Oct. 1934	Aug. 1934	July 1934	Feb. 1934	Apr. 1934
Main Contractor	L.M.S.	Drewery	Hunslet	Hunslet	Hunslet	Hunslet	Hudswell	Harland & Wolff	Armstrong	English Electric
Engine Maker	Paxman	Allen	M.A.N.	McLaren Benz	Brotherhood	Paxmen	Mirrlees	Burmeister	Sulzer	English Electric
H.P.	400	160	150	150	150	180	150	175	250	300
Speed r.p.m.	750	1200	900	1000	1200	900	1000	1100	775	600
Transmission	Hydrostatic	Gearbox Hydraulic Coupling	Gearbox Mechanical Clutch	Gearbox Mechanical Clutch	Gearbox Hydraulic Coupling	Gearbox Hydraulic Coupling	Gearbox Hydraulic Coupling	Gearbox Hydraulic Coupling	Electric	Electric
Wheelbase	15′ 8″	7′ 0″	8′ 0″	9′ 0″	9′ 0″	9′ 0″	9′ 0″	12′ 0″	13′ 0″	11′ 6″
Wheel Diameter	55″	36″	36″	40″	40″	40″	40″	38″	42″	48½″
Total Weight Tons	46	25·4	21	26.6	26	30.5	30.5	28	40.5	47

the fray, a somewhat embittered man, I am sorry to say. His lower power mechanically driven units were not therefore immediately followed up, but that they were on the right lines for lower grade duties is supported by the orders for over 500 similar machines which were one day placed by British Railways.

The 350-h.p. shunter on the other hand sold itself at once. Its advantage over steam was not only demonstrable in figures, but obvious in solid fact to all who had to do with the locomotives out in the yards. For duties rostered to give over 6,000 hours shunting per annum, a saving of 4s. 6d. per shunting hour at current values, or 45% over steam costs, was ascertained with single manning, and even with two men on the footplate, savings were still 1s. 9½d. per hour. The triumph of the diesel electric shunter was therefore firmly established, and it was the intention of the company to build no more steam, but to acquire 100 more diesels for the intensively worked yard over the period 1947 to 1952.

Although both the L.N.E. and the Southern were contemplating such a move, it was again the L.M.S. which pioneered the introduction of diesel traction for main line duties. Towards the end of his time Fairburn had discussed with Messrs. B.T.H. a 1,500-h.p. locomotive with Paxman engine which would undertake the same work as the 2–6–4 Tank Engine. By the beginning of 1946 Ivatt was in touch with three firms, B.T.H., Crompton Parkinson and English Electric who were already developing ideas for the export market. By May he had decided that the most direct way of obtaining something to run on rails in quick time was to organise a co-operative effort with a single firm, and English Electric was chosen. On May 20th, 1946, preliminary negotiations were cemented at a meeting at Stafford with Sir George Nelson, as he then was, at which I was also present. This joint effort went like clockwork, and Coleman's staff at Derby made an excellent job of the mechanical parts design, which from the first gave great satisfaction. The resulting Nos. 10000 and 10001 of 1,600 h.p. each have often been illustrated and described. On December 8th, 1947, Ivatt had the thrill of driving the first British main line diesel out of the Derby paint shop (Plate 53), while on the 16th of the same month we all accompanied it on its first run to London and thence to its secure place in history.

The remaining part of this motive power trial, namely the design and building of an 800-h.p. diesel-electric for secondary services, was entrusted to the North British Locomotive Company at an initiatory meeting in Glasgow on September 10th, 1946, using a

Paxman engine and B.T.H. electrical equipment. This locomotive was not completed before the end of the L.M.S. railway.

With these diesels, and the high level to which steam locomotive improvements had been brought, the L.M. was well poised to gather factual operating experience for the definition of future traction policy. In a report to management which was given some publicity at the beginning of 1947 it was stated " If any departure from the simple, cheap, rugged and reliable steam locomotive of normal aspect is to be envisaged for the sake of higher thermal efficiency, or for still higher availability, then the L.M.S. believes that a complete break away from steam towards diesel traction is the step which ought to be taken ". Brave words, and prophetic too, but there was yet another stage to intervene before their fulfilment.

We have now come to the end of an era. The existence of the four group companies was terminated by Act of Parliament on December 31st, 1947. Under Nationalisation which followed the future of locomotive development, whatever form it took, was bound to be different. So far as the L.M.S. is concerned we have traced the effects of the 1923 amalgamation through a chaos of conflicting interests to simple clarity of purpose, from Fowler, Anderson and E. J. H. Lemon, shading off to Stanier, Fairburn and Ivatt (Plate 52). We have seen the design pendulum swing to and fro between seeking the current best, and imposing a personal best, and we have seen how, with whatever stops and starts and even backslidings, the art of locomotive design has progressed in performance potentials, in efficiency, in reliable steam production, and in the raising of servicing and maintenance standards. So great indeed had been the improvement in boiler design and construction that the condition of this member no longer controlled shopping periods, and it became able to outlast two or more successive repairs of the engine chassis. Hotboxes, broken tyres, constricted steam flow and internal leakage had, for all practical purposes, vanished. On the other hand there was some unfinished business.

We had not succeeded in making the ' Pacifics ' fit for a reliable 100,000 miles per annum, wherever operating rosters would permit, although there were great hopes that the special features of Nos. 6256 and 6257 would make this possible. Notwithstanding much investigation, the way was not yet clear to obtaining reliable service from laminated springs, and frame fracture continued as a lively demon. The effect of the latter was mitigated, but not exorcised, by the provision for a number of locomotive types of spare

Table XIII. New Steam Locomotives added to L.M.S. stock during eight years 1940–1947 (incl.)

			1940	*1941*	*1942*	*1943*	*1944*	*1945*	*1946*	*1947*	*Total*
Stanier Designs											
Class 7		Princess Coronation	5	—	—	4	4	—	3	1	17
Class 5		2 cyl. Mixed Traffic	—	—	—	20	69	72	59	50	270
Class 4	2–6–4	2 cyl. Taper Boiler Tank	1	9	8	2	—	—	—	—	20
Class 8	2–8–0	2 cyl. Freight	53	14	68	155	165	70	—	—	525
		Total Stanier	59	23	76	181	238	142	62	51	832
Fairburn & Ivatt Designs											
Class 4	2–6–4	Fairburn 2 cyl. Taper Boiler Tank	—	—	—	—	—	45	47	38	130
Class 2	2–6–2	Ivatt Mixed Traffic Tank	—	—	—	—	—	—	10	—	10
Class 2	2–6–0	Ivatt Mixed Traffic	—	—	—	—	—	—	10	10	20
Class 4	2–6–0	Ivatt Mixed Traffic	—	—	—	—	—	—	—	3	3
		Total Fairburn Ivatt	—	—	—	—	—	45	67	51	163
Pre-Stanier Designs											
Class 4	0–6–0	Supr. Freight	8	2	—	—	—	—	—	—	10
		Total Pre-Stainer	8	2	—	—	—	—	—	—	10
		GRAND TOTAL	67	25	76	181	238	187	129	102	1005

frames complete for exchanging for defective ones at shop repairs. Enough had been learned to provide adequate lateral control for the avoidance of derailment due to the building up of periodic sinusoidal movements when track conditions were unfavourable, but rough and uncomfortable, as distinct from unsafe, riding was still all too prevalent. Yet again, we were still far from obtaining the expected benefits from the large expenditure on water treatment which had been initiated in the mid-thirties, and a full understanding of the air/gas/steam combustion relationship awaited the advent of testing equipment and technique not as yet available.

This was the state of the art when Roland Bond, Ernest Pugson and I took train on the last day of the year, to join Robin Riddles' team at Marylebone, and to enter the new world of Nationalisation, as uncharted in its own way as the world of amalgamation we had entered a quarter of a century before.

Index

LOCOMOTIVES

MISCELLANEOUS

PERSONALITIES

(The occupations indicated are those held at the time of reference in the text)